بسم الله الرحمن الرحيم

Reflections of Allah's Love

A Portrait of His Eminence

IMĀM AHMAD RAZĀ KHĀN AL-QĀDIRĪ

A Towering Figure in the Annals of Religious Revival

By Maryam Qadri

AL-MUKHTĀR BOOKS

Reflections of Allah's Love © 2012 by Maryam Qadri

No part of this book may be used or reproduced in any form without written permission, except in critical articles and reviews.

Published by:
Al-Mukhtār Books, US
PO Box 219 | Martinsville
62442
info@almukhtarbooks.com

Library of Congress Control Number: 2012941997
ISBN: 978-0-9831488-4-5

Please visit www.almukhtarbooks.com for more titles by and about the great Reviver of Islam, Imām Ahmad Razā Khān al-Qādirī ﷺ.

Allah, the Most Gracious, the Most Merciful
in Whose Name we begin

All praise belongs to Allah alone, Who perfected His religion and completed His favor upon us. May the choicest blessings and salutations of peace be upon the Messenger of Allah (*Rasūlu'llāh*), the Chief of the Envoys (*Sayyid al-Mursalīn*), and the Seal of the Prophets (*Khātam an-Nabiyyīn*), our Master Muhammad, through whom He guided us out of error, and upon his noble Family, his illustrious Companions, and those who ally themselves with him.

This work is humbly dedicated to my honorable Murshid al-Kāmil, Hazrat 'Allāma Pīrzada Mawlānā Chaman Qadri, may Allah Most High sanctify his lofty secret and grant him a long life.

Āmīn

قُلْ إِن كُنتُمْ تُحِبُّونَ ٱللَّهَ فَٱتَّبِعُونِى يُحْبِبْكُمُ ٱللَّهُ وَيَغْفِرْ لَكُمْ ذُنُوبَكُمْ ۗ وَٱللَّهُ غَفُورٌ رَّحِيمٌ ۝

Say (O beloved Prophet ﷺ, to mankind): "If you love Allah, follow me, and Allah will love you, and forgive you your sins; Allah is Ever-Forgiving, Most Merciful." (al-Qur'ān, 3:31)

Contents

Acknowledgements	ix
Preface	xiii

1.	The Razā Household: A Spiritual Legacy	1
2.	A Child is Born	10
3.	A Remarkable Youth	15
4.	The Muftī of Bareilly	20
5.	The Life of a Householder	28
6.	The Abode of Great Saints	48
7.	Journey to the Holy House	60
8.	'Allāma Naqī's Union ؓ	73
9.	The Birth of a Walī ؓ	75
10.	A Towering Figure	88
11.	Regard for Women	101
12.	A Red-Letter Day	129
13.	Political Unrest in British India	138
14.	Glad Tidings	155

Al-Arba'īn	160
Milestones in the Life of A'lā Hazrat ؓ	172

Acknowledgments

This biography was made possible thanks to the research of innumerable scholars, who have worked tirelessly to preserve and disseminate the teachings of Imām Ahmad Razā Khān ؓ in the English language. Chief among them is Mawlānā Muhammad Afthab Cassim al-Qādirī Radawī Nūrī of Imām Mustafā Research Centre in Durban (South Africa), whose comprehensive and holistic biography, *Imam Ahmad Raza: His Academic & Spiritual Services* forms the basis of this book. It is an indispensable resource and a must-read for all lovers of A'lā Hazrat.[1] Similarly the works translated by the President of Imām Ahmad Razā Academy, Shaykh Abū Muhammad 'Abdul Hādī al-Qādirī Radawī Nūrī, are a source of immense benefit, guidance, and light.

I also wish to thank Dr. Ghūlām Jīlānī for encouraging me to write this biography in accordance with the wishes of our honorable Murshid al-Kāmil, Hazrat 'Allāma Pīrzada Mawlānā Chaman Qadri (may Allah preserve

---

[1] Imām Ahmad Razā Khān is referred to by many South Asian Muslims as A'lā Hazrat (or, "The Great Presence").

him). Hazrat Sāhib is the one who established our irreplaceable link to al-Ghawth al-A'zam Sultān al-Awliyā' Sayyidunā ash-Shaykh Muhyi'd-dīn 'Abdul Qādir al-Jīlānī al-Hasanī al-Husainī ؓ, and personally encouraged this little one to take knowledge from Imām Ahmad Razā Khān al-Qādirī ؓ and start Al-Mukhtār Books.

To ensure excellence, a manuscript usually requires a team of skilled professionals who will undertake the tedious chore of proofreading it for spelling, grammar, logic, style, consistency, and appropriate expression. I have been fortunate enough to work with such a team, and its lead member, Mahomed Yunus 'Abdul Karrīm al-Qādirī has been a mentor to me throughout the course of our acquaintance. The other members of this group are dedicated adherents of the *Maslak*, literally "Way" of Imām Ahmad Razā Khān ؓ, which includes Shakil Ahmed[2] and Irfan Edhi of Medina the Illumined. I have also sought the counsel of Mawlānā Muhammad Kalīm al-Qādirī of Maktab-e Qadriah in Bolton (UK),[3] Junaid

---

[2] Shakil Ahmed created the Sunni Way website (thesunniway.com) which introduces English-speaking Muslims to the *Maslak* of Imām Ahmad Razā Khān ؓ.

[3] Mawlānā Muhammad Kalīm al-Qādirī is a leading Islamic scholar, translator, and educator in the United Kingdom. At present, he is offering weekly lessons (*Dars*) at Masjid-e Noor-ul-Islam in Bolton on Imām 'Abdul Wahhāb al-Sha'rānī's ؓ glorious masterpiece, *Lawāqih al-Anwār al-Qudsīyyah fī Bayān al-'Uhūd al-Muhammadīyyah* [The

Acknowledgements

Mohammed of Ihsanica Media in Durban,[4] and my husband, Professor Ghūlām Dastagīr, a brilliant writer who has been my greatest support and unfailing guide. He also helped me design the cover of this book which features a floral motif from the Tāj Mahal.

In Islamic art and architecture, flowers are seen as symbols of Paradise. And the king of flowers in the Qādirī Tarīqah is the rose. According to a popular narrative, the rose was Sayyidunā ash-Shaykh Muhyi'd-dīn 'Abdul Qādir al-Jīlānī's ﷺ favorite flower. The rose is also lovely, beautiful, fragrant, and soft. It reminds us that a believer should be outwardly beautiful and inwardly sweet, yet capable of guarding his natural state (*Fitra*), as a rose is adorned with thorns to safeguard it from harmful creatures.

The rose is symbolic of His Eminence, Imām Ahmad Razā Khān al-Qādirī ﷺ, for the aforementioned reasons too. He loved for the sake of Allah the Exalted, did what was beautiful in accordance with the Prophetic Sunnah, and was spiritually fragrant and genteel with the believers. He also taught the Community of Sayyidunā

Enrichment of Divine Lights in Elucidating the Muhammadan Covenants]. Seekers of knowledge can download pervious classes at http://www.noorulislambolton.com/audio.asp?optSpeaker=37.

[4] Ihsanica Media is a small, non-profit Islamic publisher founded in 2010 by individuals with a shared interest in Sacred Knowledge and spirituality (http://ihsanica.com/).

Muhammad ﷺ to safeguard their natural state of faith (*Fitra*) from irreligious reformers. It is further said that when one smells a rose he should think of our Master, the Messenger of Allah ﷺ, and he should send blessings and salutations upon the noble Prophet ﷺ (*Salawāt*). Imām Ahmad ؓ is certainly a rose from the sublime garden of the Beloved of the Lord of all worlds ﷺ.

Any error found within the pages of this book is the author's alone. As such, it would be greatly appreciated if the reader would report any and all mistakes to ensure that these blemishes do not appear in forthcoming editions.

May Allah Most Pure bless the righteous servants of the *Ahl al-Sunnah wa al-Jamā'ah* and gift them ample reward, Āmīn.

Preface

Most English biographies on the life of Imām Ahmad Razā Khān ﷺ primarily focus on his polemical works. But with polemics, inevitably, there is disputation. Such works have the latent potential of casting a negative light upon their subject due to the nature of argumentation itself. Hence the Proof of Islam,[5] Imām Abū Hāmid al-Ghazzālī ﷺ (d. 505 AH/1111 CE), said in his celebrated *Ihyā' 'Ulūm ad-Dīn*, "To make faith strong by argumentation is like striking a tree with a hot iron."[6] Although the polemic *is* necessary; it has been emphasized almost to the exclusion of all else. Thus, it seemed imperative that a non-litigious approach be taken on his life and works, one that would cultivate love for this venerable Imām by focusing on who he was behind all of his scholasticism and legal edicts (*Fatāwā*).

Reflections of Allah's Love was written with the intention of shedding light on the nobility, self-mastery, spiritual

---

[5] Hujjat al-Islām
[6] Imām al-Ghazzālī, *Revival of Religious Learning* (Karachi: Darul-Ishāt, 1993), trans. Fazlul Karim, 1:102.

excellence, and God-consciousness of Imām Ahmad Razā Khān al-Qādirī ﷺ. Included in this biographical narrative are anecdotes, excerpts, and forty narrations (*Ahādīth al-Arba'īn*) that the Imām personified. These narrations corroborate his steadfast adherence to Islam and the Sunnah. They also serve to remind us how important it is to follow the path of truth and guidance, light and radiance. To apply and experience what we learn from the life of A'lā Hazrat ﷺ is to honor him.

The Razā Household:
A Spiritual Legacy

Rarely do we come across people who have the courage to withstand the onslaught of temptation, oppression, and evil. Such spiritual cowardice is a virulent disease that must be answered through struggle (*Mujāhada*). However, it also demands the presence of an exemplar: One who is capable of leading others safely along the Straight Path and adheres strictly to the Qur'ān and the Prophetic Sunnah. Perhaps that is why the Bountiful Lord sent a family of Gnostics (*'Ārifīn*) to reside amongst the people of Bareilly, India. Men so steeped in the love of Allah that their names would become famous throughout the lands of Islam and beyond. They were born and raised in the state of Uttar Pradesh (UP) in the northern part of India, a region that boasts famous Mughal cities like Lucknow and Agra, home of the Tāj Mahal.

Reflections of Allah's Love

These outstanding scholar-saints reawakened the Sunni masses and gave them hope in the face of fear. The fountainhead of this altogether preeminent family was Mawlānā Razā 'Alī Khān an-Naqshbandī ﷺ (d. 1282/1866), a student of 'Allāma Khalīlrur Rahmān Rampurī ﷺ. He was educated at Tonk, the only Muslim state in central India, and returned home to Bareilly at the age of twenty-three.[7] He was a sagacious Gnostic (*'Ārif*),[8] who engaged in the greater *jihād* by restraining his lower self (*Nafs*) from sins, dubious matters, and excess in permissible pleasures.

Mawlānā Razā 'Alī Khān ﷺ was also a valiant freedom fighter, who served under the command of General Bakht Khān and fought the lesser *jihād* against the British. He resigned from soldiering to fully dedicate his life to attaining the highest form of knowledge (*Ma'rifa*),[9] and waging the most perfect form of struggle (*Jihād al-Akbar*). After the Revolt of 1857 ended in defeat, the "British Rāj" consolidated its authority over the vast tracks of India.[10]

---

[7] Usha Sanyal, *Ahmad Riza Khan Barelwi: In the Path of the Prophet* (Oxford: Oneworld Publications, 2005), 52-53.

[8] In point of fact, he was considered by many to be the Crown of the Gnostics (*Tāj al-'Ārifīn*).

[9] *Ma'rifa*: Direct experience of Allah, the Sublime and Exalted.

[10] British rule of the Subcontinent "officially" began in 1858 and ended in 1947 with the creation of two states, India and Pakistan. However prior to this, the East India Company had systematically consolidated its authority over most of the Subcontinent from 1757 to 1858. The Indo-

The Razā Household

This meant that most of the Community (*Umma*) was on the back-foot. But not Mawlānā Razā ﷺ; he feared no one, save Allah Most High. This astonishing fact has been documented by the King of the 'Ulamā,[11] Muftī Muhammad Zafar ad-Dīn Biharī ﷺ, who relates the following miracle (*Karāmāt*) about Mawlānā Sāhib in volume one of his *Hayāt-e A'lā Hazrat* [The Life of A'lā Hazrat]:

"After the tumult of 1857, the British tightened the reins of power and committed atrocities toward the people, and everybody went about feeling scared. Important people left their homes and went back to their villages. But Maulana Riza 'Alī Khan continued to live in his house as before, and would go to the mosque five times a day to say his prayers in congregation. One day some Englishmen passed by the mosque, and decided to see if anyone was inside so they could catch hold of them and beat them up. They went inside and looked around but didn't see anyone. Yet the Maulana was there at the time. Allah had made them blind, so they would be unable to see him. ... [When] he came out of the

---

Pak region spent almost two-hundred years under the yoke of British colonialism.
[11] Mālik al-'Ulamā

mosque, they were still watching out for people, but no one saw him (Bihari, 1938: 5)."¹²

Allah Most High says: *And We shall raise a barrier in front of them and a barrier behind them, and cover them over so they will not be able to see.*¹³

Mawlānā Razā 'Alī Khān ﷺ instilled in his line characteristic Islamic virtues such as God-consciousness (*Taqwā*), Patience (*Sabr*), Contentment (*Ridā*), Spiritual Courtesy (*Ādāb*), Scrupulousness (*Wara'*), Compassion, Sincerity (*Ikhlās*), Courage, Steadfastness (*Istiqamāh*), and Faith (*Īmān*). His son, 'Allāma Naqī 'Alī Khān ﷺ (d. 1297/1880), was greatly endowed with these precious gifts. The latter was given the title *Ra'īs al-Muhaqqiqīn* (or, "Leader of the Realizers") by their contemporaries.

Like his father before him, 'Allāma Naqī ﷺ was a sincere and compassionate teacher (*Mudarris*) that bid his devoted students to always remember that "excess *is* excess."¹⁴ He further warned that greed is a serious

---

¹² Sanyal, *Ahmad Riza Khan Barelwi*, 51.
¹³ Al-Qur'ān, 36:9.
¹⁴ 'Allāma Naqī 'Alī Khān, "The Excellence of Knowledge and the 'Ulamā" in *Thesis of Imam Ahmad Raza* ﷺ (Durban: Barkātur-Razā Publications, 2005), trans. Shaykh 'Abdul Hādī, 4:27.

The Razā Household

obstacle on the path, since the desire for more is generally found in every human being. And insatiable greed has devoured many, whose gross consumption consumed them. Thus, he counseled his students to earn (or obtain) that which suffices their basic needs, and nothing more.[15] This is echoed in the supplication (*Du'ā*) of Prophet 'Īsā ibn Maryam ﷺ:[16] *Give us our (daily) bread, for You are the best of all givers of food.*[17] It also conforms perfectly to the guidance of Allah's Messenger ﷺ, who said: **"Richness does not lie in many possessions; richness is the richness of the soul."**[18]

'Allāma Naqī ؓ would affectionately smile in reply to his students, especially when they posed an intricate question to him. They would pose such questions in a spirited attempt to outwit their teacher, but to no avail![19] Their *Mudarris* was an *'Allāma*, literally "an encyclopedia of knowledge," that always left them speechless.

In 1878, 'Allāma Naqī ؓ became a disciple (*Murīd*) and deputy (*Khalīfah*) of Sayyid Shāh Āl-e Rasūl Marehrawī ؓ, the celebrated Hadīth expert (*Muhaddīth*) whose chain of

---

[15] 'Allāma Naqī 'Alī Khān, "The Excellence of Knowledge and the 'Ulamā" in *Thesis of Imam Ahmad Raza* ؓ, 4:27.
[16] Jesus, the son of Mary ﷺ
[17] Al-Qur'ān, 5:114.
[18] Ibn Hajar al-'Asqalānī, *Selections from the Fath al-Bārī* (Bartlow: The Muslim Academic Trust, 2009), trans. Abdal Hakim Murad, 8.
[19] 'Allāma Naqī 'Alī Khān, "The Excellence of Knowledge and the 'Ulamā" in *Thesis of Imam Ahmad Raza* ؓ, 4:3.

transmission passes through Shāh 'Abdul 'Azīz son of Shāh Walī Allah ﷺ. He also received authorization (*Ijāzat*) to narrate Hadīth from the Preceptor (*Ustād*) of the 'Ulamā, the Shaykh of the Sanctuary, Sayyid Ahmad Zayni Dahlān Makkī ﷺ in 1879 in Mecca the Ennobled.

He authored a number of texts defending Islamic orthodoxy and laid the foundation stone of Darul Iftā,[20] Bareilly. Imām Ahmad Razā Khān ﷺ in *al-Malfūz al-Sharīf* [The Noble Vocals] relates the following story about his father, which reflects one of his spiritual gifts and the station (*Maqām*) he attained:

> "[In a dream] Mawlānā Barkāt Ahmad ﷺ accompanied my father ('Allāma Naqī ﷺ) who came to visit me during an illness. They asked me how I was feeling.
>
> I replied: 'I am exhausted from the severity of my illness, so please make *Du'ā* for me to now leave this world (*Dunyā*) with faith (*Īmān*).' Upon hearing this, my father's face turned red. In response to my request, he said: 'There are still fifty-two years in Medina the Illumined.' Allah the Exalted knows best what he was referring to. I

---

[20] *Darul Iftā*: An office of Islamic jurisprudence where people visit or send questions on all aspects of the Sacred Law.

couldn't understand the meaning of his enigmatic statement.

Later in my life, the interpretation of this dream unfolded. I was fifty-two years old during my second trip to the Sacred Sanctuary (*Haram*). Actually, my [exact] age was fifty-one years and five months. My father ﷺ had foretold of this trip fourteen years ago [in the aforementioned dream]. Allah Most High entrusts knowledge of the unseen (*'Ilm al-Ghayb*) to the servants of our Master, the Messenger of Allah ﷺ, and Wahhābīs [have the audacity to] reject the Beloved Prophet's knowledge of the unseen ﷺ.

A few years ago in the month of Rajab, I dreamt of my father, who said: 'You will fall very sick this Ramadan, but you must not leave the fast.' It happened just as he predicted. The doctors tried in vain to dissuade me from fasting, but I ignored their wishes. By the Grace of Allah the Exalted I kept my entire fast and fully recovered. There is a noble utterance (*Hadīth Sharīf*) that clearly states: **'Fast and you will get well.'**"[21]

---

[21] Imām Mustafā Razā Khān, *al-Malfūz al-Sharīf* (Durban: Barkātur-Razā Publications, 2007), trans. Shaykh 'Abdul Hādī, 2:191-192.

Reflections of Allah's Love

The Mālikī jurist and Qur'ān commentator of Spain, al-Qurtubī ☙, confirms this: "The truthful, righteous Muslim (*al-muslim al-sadiq al-salih*) is he whose state matches that of prophets and thereby is bestowed (*ukrima*) some of the same kind of gifts they were given: that is to behold the unseen (*wa huwa al-ittila ala al-ghayb*)."[22] All praise belongs to Allah alone! The Sublime Lord revealed to His Messenger ☙ the following verse regarding His saints (*Awlīyā*): *All bounties are in the Hands of Allah: He grants them to whom He pleases!*[23] And no doubt both Mawlānā Razā ☙ and his illustrious son, 'Allāma Naqī ☙, were the beneficiaries of such bounties. This will be clear from the following episode, with which we shall conclude this chapter.

When it came to interpreting dreams, Mawlānā Razā 'Alī Khān ☙ was an adept, his correct interpretation of one of 'Allāma Naqī's ☙ auspicious dreams that transpired a year before the Indian Revolt, is spiritually significant and of great relevance to our subject. After listening to the highlights of his son's dream, Mawlānā Razā ☙ perceptively said: "This

---

[22] Al-Qurtubī as quoted by Imām Ibn Hajar al-'Asqalānī in his *Fath al-Bārī* [Victory of the Creator]. This quote was excerpted from *al-Musuat al-islami aqida ahl al-sunnah wa al-jamaat* (Mountain View: As-Sunna Foundation of America, 1998), 3:108.
[23] Al-Qur'ān, 3:73.

The Razā Household

dream indicates that you are going to be the father of a child—a boy—who will grow up to be pious and knowledgeable. His name will gain prominence from East to West."[24] And so it came to be. In 1856, 'Allāma Naqī's wife ﷺ gave birth to a radiant baby boy, who would grow to become a towering figure in the annals of Islamic revival.

When one is in the company of Allah's Friends even advanced medical science looks positively primitive. For this reason among other proofs, the Sufis have historically affirmed that the Prophets and Sufi saints are bestowed knowledge of the five unseen matters by Allah Most Pure.[25] This includes, of course, knowledge of what is in the wombs.

What follows is a portrait of His Eminence, Imām Ahmad Razā Khān al-Qādirī ﷺ, the son and grandson of two who attained, and one of the most famous scholar-saints of modern times.

---

[24] Mawlānā Muhammad Afthab Cassim, *Imam Ahmad Raza: His Academic & Spiritual Services*, accessed on August 18, 2011, http://www.noori.org/Books/ImamAhmedRaza.pdf, 10.

[25] Al-Qur'ān, 31:34. For further discussion of this topic, see Shaykh Monawwar Ateeq, "Knowledge of the Unseen Theology: Arguments on the Scope of Prophetic Knowledge."

A Child is Born

According to traditional sources, the noble Prophet Muhammad ﷺ was born on a Monday, and he used to fast on this day to commemorate his blessed birth (*Mawlid*) every week. Imām Ahmad Razā Khān ؓ was also born on a Monday at the time of Zuhr in 1272/1856. It seems befitting that Allah the Exalted would send a Renewer (*Mujaddid*) to this world, who would defend the honor of His Beloved Messenger ﷺ, on the day of Mawlid. His birth not only occurred on a virtuous day,[26] but also at the time of prayer!

It was a Razā family tradition to name each new born son Muhammad, as the Prophet ﷺ said: **"Name yourselves with my name but do not use my *kunya*."**[27] His personal name that is recognized all over the world is

---

[26] Imām 'Abdallāh ibn 'Alawī al-Haddad, *The Book of Assistance* (Louisville: Fons Vitae, 2003), trans. Mostafā al-Badawī, 73 and n59.

[27] The Prophet's *kunya* is Abu'l-Qāsim ﷺ (or, "The Father of Allotments") because he was made the distributor (*Qāsim*) to divide things between us. This Hadīth Sharīf is related by al-Bukhārī ؓ in his *al-Ādāb al-Mufrad*. The Prophet ﷺ also named his eldest son Qāsim ؓ.

A Child is Born

Ahmad Razā. It was given to him by his prescient grandfather, Mawlānā Razā 'Alī Khān ◈.

Those familiar with the religious tradition of Islam know that the Friends of Allah are often conferred many names, surnames, and titles to highlight their exalted rank. It is a mark of spiritual courtesy (*Ādāb*) to mention them by their titles followed by the appropriate benedictions. One of the many benefits of this honorific-system is that we learn a rich store of information about the Gnostics themselves from such appellations. Thus, we adhere faithfully to the words of our Lord: *And veneration are for Allah, and for His Messenger* ◈, *and for the Believers*[28] and *We exalt in degree whom We will; and above each one that hath knowledge is one that knoweth more*[29] and *Whosoever respects the Signs of Allah then it is from the piety of hearts.*[30] This is further affirmed in a holy utterance (*Hadīth Qudsī*) of Allah Most Pure spoken through the mouth of our Prophet ◈: **"Whosoever disrespects a friend (*Walī*) of Mine, I declare war on him."**[31]

---

[28] Al-Qur'ān, 63:8.
[29] Al-Qur'ān, 12:76.
[30] Al-Qur'ān, 22:32.
[31] Imām Ahmad Razā Khān, *The Pre-eminence of Sayyid 'Abd al-Qādir Jīlānī over Sayyid Ahmad Kabīr al-Rifā'i* (Durban: Barkātur-Razā Publications, 2005), trans. Shaykh 'Abdul Hādī, 38. This holy utterance is also cited in *Fath al-Bārī*, *Tadkarat al-Huffāz*, and *Siyar A'lām al-Nubala* on the authority of Abū Hurayrah ◈.

Imām Ahmad Razā ﷺ received many honorific appellations later in life that are worth noting here such as: A'lā Hazrat (or, "The Great Presence"). *Hazrat* is derived from an Arabic word that means one who is constantly in the presence of Allah. *A'lā* reinforces the ensuing title, emphasizing the profundity and magnitude of his presence above other righteous men. He was also known as "the emerald from amongst the treasures of Allah the Exalted" and "the sweet-scented rose from the fragrant garden of the Holy Prophet ﷺ."[32] The name corresponding to the year of his birth was *al-Mukhtār*, which is derived from the sum total of its letters according to the Science of Numerology (*Abjad*).[33] *Mukhtār* is an Arabic word meaning chosen, selected. In other words, he was the one selected by Allah Most High.

In after-years, Imām Ahmad Razā ﷺ was able to derive this name from the numerical value of the following Qur'ānic verse: *Thou wilt not find any people who believe in Allah and the Last Day, loving those who resist Allah and His Messenger, even though they were their fathers or their sons, or their brothers, or their kindred. For such He has written faith in their hearts, and strengthened them with a spirit from*

---

[32] Mawlānā Muhammad Afthab Cassim, *The Chain of Light* (Durban: Imam Mustafa Research Center, 2008), 2:93.

[33] *Alif* (1) + *lām* (30) + *mīm* (40) + *khā* (600) + *tā* (400) + *alif* (1) + *rā* (200) = 1272 AH.

A Child is Born

Himself. And He will admit them to Gardens beneath which rivers flow, to dwell therein (forever). Allah will be well pleased with them, and they with Him. They are the party of Allah. Truly it is the party of Allah that will achieve felicity.[34]

Top-ranking muftīs and scholars from Mecca the Ennobled conferred the following titles upon Imām Ahmad Razā Khān ﷺ: "The Coolness of the Scholars' Eyes" (*Qurratu 'Ayun al-'Ulamā*), "The Beloved and Accepted Slave of Allah," "The Seal of the Realizers" (*Khātam al-Muhaqqiqīn*), "The Leader of the Islamicists" (*Sayyid al-'Ulamā*), and "The Renewer of the Twentieth Century" (*Mujaddid al-Mi'ah al-Hadirah*)!

Noble dignitaries from the illumined city of Medina declared him to be: "The Leader of the Imāms" (*Imām al-A'immah*), "The Leader of the Mystics" (*Imām al-Sufiyah*), "The Pride of the Righteous Forebearers and the Forthcoming 'Ulamā" (*Fakhr al-Salaf wal Khalaf*), "The Renewer of the Community" (*Mujaddid hadhihil Umma*), "The Judge of the Judges" (*Qadi'l Qudat*), "The Imām of the Hadīth Masters" (*Imām al-Muhaddithīn*), "The Vanquisher of Innovation and the Upholder of the Sunnah" (*Mahiy al-Bid'ah, Hamiy al-Sunnah*), and "The Renewer of the Twentieth Century" (*Mujaddid al-Qarn*).

Other titles include: "The Greatest Shaykh" (*Shaykh al-Akbar*), "The Shaykh of Islam" (*Shaykh al-Islām*), and "The

---

[34] Al-Qur'ān, 58:22.

Glory of the Religion" (*Zia ad-Dīn*). Such was his fame and repute among the pious servants (*Sālihīn*) of the Meccan and Medinan Sanctuaries (*Haramayn*).[35] But the name that Imām Ahmad Razā Khān ؓ chose for himself was "Servant of the Chosen One ﷺ" (*'Abdul Mustafā* ﷺ) to signify his ardent devotion and reverential love for Allah's Messenger ﷺ. Most of his correspondence and legal edicts were signed with this name, because it conveys unequivocally his complete self-effacement in the Beloved of the Lord of all worlds ﷺ.

---

[35] These titles are recorded in his most celebrated works like *al-Fuyuzāt al-Makkiyya*, *Husām al-Haramayn*, and *ad-Dawlah al-Makkiyyah*, which received commendations from leading Sunni scholars.

A Remarkable Youth

"This dream indicates that you are going to be the father of a child—a boy—who will grow up to be pious and knowledgeable. His name will gain prominence from East to West."[36] The perceptive words of Mawlānā Razā 'Alī Khān ؓ proved true, and the prodigious nature of the child was evident even in the earliest years. At the age of three his grandson was seen outside of the Razā Mosque speaking a mellifluous Arabic to a stranger dressed in traditional Arabian attire.[37] A year later, this same child had already taken to heart the Prophet's words ﷺ: "**Modesty is a branch of faith.**"[38] For when a woman of ill repute walked past him in the streets of Bareilly he immediately lifted up his kurta pajama to cover his eyes. The prostitute ridiculed him by saying: "You covered your eyes, but allowed your *satr*[39] to be shown," to which he

---

[36] Mawlānā Muhammad Afthab Cassim, *Imam Ahmad Raza*, 10.
[37] Ibid., 14-15. The mysterious stranger was never seen again in the locality!
[38] This Hadīth Sharīf is narrated by al-Bukhārī ؓ and Muslim ؓ.
[39] *Satr*: The area or part of the body that must be covered with appropriate clothing.

profoundly replied: "When the eyes are tempted, then the heart becomes tempted. When the heart is tempted, then the concealed parts become tempted." The woman was so affected by his speech that she fell unconscious.[40]

Modesty is an Islamic virtue that entails more than just covering the physical frame, it also comprises of guarding the heart from external stimuli to the greatest extent possible. Ahmad Razā could not cover the woman so he covered himself. How wisely has it been said that: "The eye is the window of the soul." The Master of Sharī'ah ﷺ has informed us that the first inadvertent glance is forgiven, but to cast a second glance is sinful.[41] Little Ahmad Razā had understood this profound teaching at the deepest levels. In this same year, he completed the recitation of the Holy Qur'ān, which is an unparalleled feat considering that most children accomplish this meritorious act during the latter part of their elementary years.[42]

When Ahmad Razā was only six years old, he stood on the pulpit and delivered a two hour extempore sermon on the blessed birth of the Messenger of Allah ﷺ during the glorious month of Rabī al-Awwal. His audience consisted

---

[40] Mawlānā Muhammad Afthab Cassim, *Imam Ahmad Raza*, 12.
[41] Muftī Jalāl ad-Dīn Ahmad al-Qādirī al-Amjadī, *In Light of the Sacred Traditions of the Beloved* ﷺ (Bolton: Maktab-e-Qadira, 2010), trans. Muhammad Kalīm al-Qādirī, 303-305.
[42] Mawlānā Muhammad Afthab Cassim, *Imam Ahmad Raza*, 18.

A Remarkable Youth

of scholars and laymen, who were enraptured by the maturity and eloquence of this lad, who increased their love for the Beloved of the Lord of all worlds ﷺ.[43] There can be no doubt that Allah fashioned him for greatness and sanctification.

Ahmad Razā ؒ wanted to keep the fast in the sacrosanct month of Ramadan. But fasting in India during the summer is especially difficult, even for adults, so his venerable father lovingly took him into a room where sweets were kept. 'Allāma Naqī ؒ closed the door and said: "Eat the sweets." But the boy affirmed that he was fasting. His father then said: "The fasting of children is always like this. The door is closed and no one is looking. Now you may eat." But his son very sweetly explained, "The One by Whose command I fast, He sees me." 'Allāma Naqī began to weep upon hearing his son's reply.[44]

Allah, the Sublime and Exalted, says: *O you who truly believe! Fasting is enjoined upon you as it was enjoined upon those before you, so that you may become pious.*[45] And what is piety (*Taqwā*)? *Taqwā* is God-consciousness, one of the most highly praised human qualities in the Holy Qur'ān, which is closely connected to *Ihsān*, perfection of belief

---

[43] Mawlānā Muhammad Afthab Cassim, *Imam Ahmad Raza*, 13.
[44] Ibid.
[45] Al-Qur'ān, 2:183.

and practice. In the above anecdote Imām Ahmad Razā ﷺ gave us a classic example of *Taqwā*. He hadn't even reached the age of accountability, yet he left his appetite, his food and drink purely for the sake of Allah. His deed beautifully conformed to a holy utterance (*Hadīth Qudsī*) of Allah Himself reported by the Blessed Prophet ﷺ, **"Allah the Exalted has said: 'All good deeds of the son of Adam are multiplied ten to seven hundredfold, except fasting, for it is Mine, and I shall reward a man for it, for he has left his appetite, his food and drink for My sake!'"**[46]

This exceptional child possessed more knowledge and insight than most people exhibit in their lifetimes. When he was eight years old he wrote a statement on obligatory duties. His beloved father (who was a celebrated Muftī) looked at the boy's report and said: "If only an adult could answer in this fashion."[47] On another occasion, 'Allāma Naqī ﷺ was teaching his son *I'lm al-Thubūt*, on the margins of this book he had written some objections and answers. Ahmad Razā ﷺ carefully examined the book and wrote an in-depth footnote that ruled out the need for an objection. Later his noble father discovered this footnote and stood up out of elation, held his son to his breast, and

---

[46] Imām 'Abdallāh ibn 'Alawī al-Haddad, *The Book of Assistance*, 73.
[47] Mawlānā Muhammad Afthab Cassim, *Imam Ahmad Raza*, 14.

A Remarkable Youth

declared: "Ahmad Razā! You do not learn from me, but you teach me."[48] The lad was a youth of ten at the time.

At the age of thirteen he completed the Dars-e Nizāmī syllabus studying a range of twenty-one Islamic sciences. This year also marked the beginning of his *fatāwā* writing. His first legal edict (*Fatwā*) was on fosterage.[49] 'Allāma Naqī ﷺ was so impressed with the verdict that he immediately entrusted his son with the weighty task of issuing religious edicts at Darul Iftā, Bareilly.

---

[48] Mawlānā Muhammad Afthab Cassim, *Imam Ahmad Raza*, 14.
[49] Ibid., 19.

The Muftī of Bareilly

During the years when A'lā Hazrat ﷺ was still a mere youth, a judicial decree (*Fatwā*) was issued that became a topic of much discussion in Uttar Pradesh. The legal edict given by Mawlānā Irshād Husain Mujaddidī ﷺ had been endorsed by several 'Ulamā, but the matter remained inconclusive and a second opinion was sought. A messenger was duly sent to 'Allāma Naqī 'Alī ﷺ for his expert opinion regarding this edict. Instead of opining upon the issue himself, the great savant deferred to an esteemed scholar in an adjoining room, and directed the messenger to him. Much to the messenger's surprise however, he found the designated room occupied by a "rather young man," who, in his eyes, did not seem capable of handling such delicate matters. Naturally, the messenger sought his way back to 'Allāma Naqī quite confused and thinking that a mistake had been made. Imām Ahmad Razā ﷺ, the "young man" in the adjacent room, was only twenty years old at the time, and the messenger, no doubt, expected to meet with a senior scholar (or, *Molvī Sāhib*) of an advanced age which might

The Muftī of Bareilly

have been more qualified to comment upon this particular case.[50]

Once again 'Allāma Naqī ﷺ instructed the messenger to take the question to his son, who upon receiving it, found that the said verdict, given by Mawlānā Irshād Husain ﷺ was in fact incorrect. Imām Ahmad Razā ﷺ made the necessary changes and turned it over to his noble father for inspection. 'Allāma Naqī ﷺ endorsed his son's corrections, and the fatwā was then sent back to the governor of Rampur, who asked the original author, Mawlānā Irshād Husain ﷺ, for an explanation. The renowned scholar humbly admitted that his own verdict was, in fact in error, and the revision from Bareilly was quite correct. The astonished governor inquired: "If the fatwā from Bareilly is correct, then why did so many 'Ulamā verify and endorse your answer?" Mawlānā Irshād Husain ﷺ replied: "They endorsed my verdict, because I am a prominent scholar, but the true verdict is the one written by the Muftī of Bareilly."[51]

After learning that the Muftī of Bareilly was only twenty years old, the governor's surprise was all the more and he longed to meet the young jurist. His wish was granted when Imām Ahmad Razā ﷺ visited Rampur. During their meeting the governor offered Imām Ahmad

---

[50] Mawlānā Muhammad Afthab Cassim, *Imam Ahmad Raza*, 21.
[51] Ibid., 21-22.

Razā ﷺ a sliver chair to sit on as a mark of respect. But he politely declined the governor's kind offer, since silver furniture is unlawful and ostentatious. Feeling a sense of shame, the rebuked governor then beseeched him to sit on his own bed and encouraged the talented Muftī to study some books on logic under the supervision of Molvī 'Abdul Haqq Khairabadī. The latter was a scholar of no meager repute and indeed prided himself for his learning. Coincidentally, it was at this precise moment that Molvī 'Abdul Haqq himself entered the room.[52]

The conversation that ensued is noteworthy and has been recorded in volume one of *Hayāt-e A'lā Hazrat* narrated by Muftī Muhammad Zafar ad-Dīn Biharī ﷺ:

"Maulana 'Abd ul-Haqq believed that there were only two and a half 'ulama in the world: one, Maulana Bahr ul-'ulama ['Abd al-'Alī of Farangi Mahall, d. 1810-11], the second, his father [Fazl-e Haqq Khairabadi, d. 1861], and the last half, himself. How could he tolerate this young boy being called an 'alim? He asked Ahmad Riza: Which is the most advanced book you have read in logic?
Ahmad Riza answered: *Qazi mubarak*.
He then asked: Have you read *Sharah tahzib*?

---

[52] Mawlānā Muhammad Afthab Cassim, *Imam Ahmad Raza*, 22.

The Muftī of Bareilly

Ahmad Riza Khān, hearing the derision in his voice, asked: Oh, do you teach *Sharah tahzib* after *Qazi mubarak* over here?
['Abd ul-Haqq decided to try a different approach. He asked:] What are you working on right now?
Ahmad Riza: Teaching, writing of fatawa, and writing.
'Abd ul-Haqq: In what field do you write?
Ahmad Riza: Legal questions (*masa'il*), religious sciences (*diniyat*), and rebuttal of Wahhabis (*radd-e wahhabiyya*).[53]
'Abd ul-Haqq: Rebuttal of Wahhabis? [A discussion about the best authority in this field of disputation followed, at the end of which 'Abd ul-Haqq fell silent.] (Bihari, 1938:33-34)"[54]

Mawlānā Muhammad Afthab Cassim relates the rest of this story in *Imām Ahmad Raza: His Academic & Spiritual Services*. He notes that when Molvī 'Abdul Haqq asked Imām Ahmad Razā ﷺ about his field of expertise, the

---

[53] The followers of Muhammad ibn 'Abdul Wahhāb (d. 1207/1792) are called Wahhābīs; they inaccurately refer to themselves as "Salafīs." Wahhābīs violently diverge from those on the Sunni path in matters of belief, methodological understanding, and traditional religious authority. For this reason refuting Wahhābīs became a dominate feature of Sunni heresiography.
[54] Sanyal, *Ahmad Riza Khan Barelwi*, 59.

latter said that he specialized in any field that was necessary at a given moment, and this included debating Wahhābīs. Molvī 'Abdul Haqq retorted: "There is a scholar from Badayun that is also into this fanaticism." He was referring to none other than Mawlānā 'Abdul Qādir ⚘. This calculated remark deeply offended Imām Ahmad Razā ⚘, who replied to Molvī 'Abdul Haqq's barb by saying: "Your father ('Allāma Fazle Haqq Khairabadī ⚘) was the first person to debate the Wahhābīs, and he wrote a book against Ismā'il ad-Dihlawī[55] entitled *Tahqīq al-Fatwā fi Ibtal al-Taghwa* [Investigating the Verdict in Refutation to the Oppressor who goes Outside the Boundaries of Islam]."[56] 'Allāma Fazle Haqq Khairabadī actually issued a fatwā of unbelief (*Kufr*) against Ismā'il ad-Dihlawī and his book *Taqwiyat al-Īmān* [Strengthening of Faith] in *Tahqīq al-Fatwā fi Ibtāl al-Taghwa* (1822). Seventeen leading scholars of the *Ahl al-Sunnah wa al-Jamā'ah* endorsed this legal edict condemning ad-Dihlawī for his deviation and heresy.[57] When the elder Khairabadī's fierce penmanship against the Wahābbīs was clearly revealed, his son (Molvī 'Abdul

---

[55] Ismā'īl ad-Dihlawī's books such as *Taqwiyat al-Īmān, Īdāh al-Haqq, al-Sirāt al-Mustaqīm*, etc. form the basis of Wahhābīsm in the Indo-Pakistanī region. He strayed far from the Sunni and Naqshbandī Sufi path of his illustrious forefathers.
[56] Mawlānā Muhammad Afthab Cassim, *Imam Ahmad Raza*, 22-23.
[57] A scan of this Urdu fatwā (accessed on August 20, 2011) is available at http://www.falaah.co.uk/refutation/wahabi/94-fatwa-upon-ismail-dehalvi-.html.

Haqq) could offer no argument, and fell silent. The tables had been turned against the "senior" Molvī in a debate that he had forced upon the young jurist from Bareilly. Undoubtedly, this was just a foretaste of what was to come from the searing blade that was Al'ā Hazrat's scholarship, which unlike other claims to learning, was a clear and sharp reflection of divinely inspired inner knowledge. A caution and guard against meaningless hairsplitting that invariably leads to heterodoxy.

Imām Ahmad Razā ؓ had immense respect for 'Allāma Fazle Haqq Khairabadī ؓ, because one of his own teachers, Mawlānā 'Abdul 'Alī Khān Rampurī ؓ, studied under him. The upshot of this discussion is that the Muftī of Bareilly decided not to study under Molvī 'Abdul Haqq, since it would be an insult to the 'Ulamā of the *Ahl al-Sunnah wa al-Jamā'ah*.[58]

All praise belongs to Allah alone, Lord of the worlds! Such devotion to *Haqq*[59] is rare indeed. According to a report from Kathīr ibn 'Abdi'llāh ibn 'Amr ibn 'Awf ؓ, on the authority of his father ؓ, who heard it from his grandfather ؓ, the latter stated that Allah's Messenger ﷺ once said: **"You must follow the exemplary traditional practices [*sunan*] of those who have gone before you, by**

---

[58] Mawlānā Muhammad Afthab Cassim, *Imam Ahmad Raza*, 22-23.
[59] *Haqq*: Truth. In this context *Haqq* also refers to 'Allāmā Fazle ؓ, whose opinion Imām Ahmad Razā ؓ respected.

treading in their very footsteps. You must take exactly the same course as the one they took, inch by inch, cubit by cubit, span by span, to the extent that if they had ever entered a lizard's lair, you would enter it too."⁶⁰ Al-Bayhaqī ؓ in his *al-Zuhd al-Kabīr* narrates that the Prophet ﷺ said: **"The keeper of my Sunnah at the time my Community has lapsed into corruption will receive the reward of a hundred martyrs."**⁶¹

Here it is worth noting that Imām Ahmad Razā ؓ also received Islamic knowledge and permission to transmit knowledge (*Ijāzat*) in Hadīth from the following luminaries:

❖ Mawlānā 'Abdul 'Alī Khān Rampurī ؓ (student of 'Allāma Fazle Haqq Khairabadī ؓ) as noted previously;

---

⁶⁰ Shaykh 'Abdul Qādir al-Jīlānī, *Sufficient Provision for Seekers of the Path of Truth* (Hollywood: Al-Baz Publishing, Inc., 1995), trans. Muhtar Holland, 1:393.

⁶¹ The reward of one martyr is admittance to Paradise without any accounting. This Hadīth Sharīf was excerpted from *The Approach of Armageddon? An Islamic Perspective* (Washington, DC: Islamic Supreme Council of America, 2003), 97.

❖ Shaykh al-Kabīr, Shāh Abu'l Husain Ahmad an-Nūrī Marehrawī ؓ (student of Mawlānā Nūr Ahmad Badayunī ؓ);

❖ Shaykh al-Tarīqah, Shāh Āl-e Rasūl Marehrawī ؓ (student of Shāh 'Abdul Azīz Muhaddīth ad-Dihlawī ؓ).

Mawlānā 'Abdul 'Alī Khān ؓ stamped his intellectual position indelibly on Imām Ahmad Razā's keen mind as the aforementioned exchange with Molvī 'Abdul Haqq clearly admits. The same is true regarding his unbreakable ties with Shaykh al-Kabīr, Sayyid Shāh Abu'l Husain Ahmad an-Nūrī Marehrawī ؓ, and Shaykh at-Tarīqah, Sayyid Shāh Āl-e Rasūl Marehrawī ؓ. But before we can discuss this inviolable relationship between Master (*Murshid*) and disciple (*Murīd*), another very important and sacred event must transpire—the young Imām's marriage (*Nikāh*).

The Life of a Householder

Allah the Exalted has said: *Marry the unwed among you.*[62] His Beloved Messenger ﷺ said: **"Marriage is my exemplary way [*sunnatī*]; whoever loves my character [*fitratī*] should follow my example."**[63] 'Abdullāh ibn 'Umar ؓ narrates that the Prophet ﷺ said: **"The world is an asset and the best asset of the world is a pious woman."**[64] Out of deference to the Revelation and the Sunnah of Allah's Messenger ﷺ, Imām Ahmad Razā ؓ married Sayyidah Irshād Begum ؓ,[65] the eldest daughter of Shaykh Afdal Husain al-'Uthmanī ؓ, in the year 1291/1874. The Imām was only eighteen years old when their marriage (*Nikāh*) took place. They were blessed with two sons and five daughters. Each birth must have been a reminder to them of our Master's ﷺ promise: **"Marry and

---

[62] Al-Qur'ān, 24:32.
[63] Imām al-Ghazzālī, *The Proper Conduct of Marriage in Islam* (Hollywood: Al-Baz Publishing, Inc., 1998), trans. Muhtar Holland, 8.
[64] Muftī Jalāl ad-Dīn Ahmad al-Qādirī al-Amjadī, *In Light of the Sacred Traditions of the Beloved* ﷺ, 294.
[65] *Begum*: Lady; queen: the title of a noblewoman which reflects her admirable stature and stately manner.

The Life of a Householder

multiply, then I shall glory in you before the nations on the Day of Resurrection: [in all of you,] even the miscarried fetus."[66] According to Imām al-Ghazzālī ☙ in his book *Ādāb an-Nikāh*, marriage is a means to five benefits: (1) children, (2) the stilling of passions, (3) good housekeeping, (4) extended family ties, and (5) spiritual training through coping with all the foregoing.[67]

When a man faithfully intends to follow the Prophet ﷺ he will naturally become an extremely thoughtful, considerate, tender, loving husband and father, as the Sublime Lord has said: *You have in the Messenger of Allah a beautiful pattern of conduct for whosoever hopes for Allah and the Last Day, and remembers Allah oft.*[68] Our Prophet ﷺ once said: **"The most perfect of the believers in faith is he who has the best character, and is most gentle toward his family."**[69] A'lā Hazrat ☙ was such a man who addressed his own self first, then his beloved family members, and lastly the Umma in general.

To better understand how he was raised and how he, in turn, raised his own children a portion of his masterpiece *Mishalah al-Irshād ila Huquq al-Awlad* [To Take the Right Course in Fulfilling the Rights of Children] is

---

[66] Imām al-Ghazzālī, *The Proper Conduct of Marriage in Islam*, 8.
[67] Ibid., 14.
[68] Al-Qur'ān, 33:21.
[69] Imām al-Ghazzālī, *The Proper Conduct of Marriage in Islam*, 63.

being presented here. What follows are fifty-two guidelines that he recorded in this irreplaceable book,[70] which highlights his views on Islamic parenting and how to raise upright children:

RIGHTS BEFORE CONCEPTION
1. It is a birth right of every Muslim child to be born to pious parents. Thus, single Muslims should not marry among irreligious and ignoble people, because immorality is handed down through socialization.
2. Recite the Name of Allah (*Bismi'llāh*) before intimacy so that Satan does not partner with the infant.
3. Do not look at a woman's private parts during intimacy, as there is a genuine fear that the child may be born blind.

THE RIGHTS OF CHILDREN FROM BIRTH TO INFANCY
4. Immediately after the birth of a child recite the call to prayer (*Adhān*) in his right ear

---

[70] Some of the points have been rearranged in accordance with the headings that were added by the author.

The Life of a Householder

and the call of assembly (*Iqāmah*) in his left ear.

5. Sweeten his mouth with honey, so that the sweet taste may sweeten his character.
6. On the seventh day, or whenever possible, sacrifice an animal on behalf of the child (*Aqiqah*).
7. Shave the child's hair from his head.
8. Weigh the child's hair and give its weight in silver to charity.
9. Rub saffron on the child's head.
10. Give the child a Muslim name such as 'Abdullāh, 'Abdul-Rahmān, Ahmad, Hāmid, Hasan, Muhyi'd-dīn, etc.
11. The mother should suckle the infant for two years or employ a pious wet-nurse, since milk affects aspects of the child's personality.
12. Children should be given lawful (*Halāl*) food from permissible earnings. Unlawful (*Harām*) food and illicit earnings breed unclean habits.
13. Recite *Allahu, Allahu* in your infant's ear, then the Kalima at-Tawhīd (*Lā ilāha illa-Allah*), and finally the full Kalima (*Lā ilāha illa-Allah, Muhammadun Rasūlu'llāh* 🌸).

14. Announce your son's circumcision.

THE RIGHTS OF CHILDREN FROM TODDLERHOOD[71] TO ADOLESCENCE[72]

15. Children are Allah's gift to parents. They must be treated with tenderness, mercy, and love. Be compassionate with them.
16. Make their hearts happy within the limits of Allah's pure law (*Sharī'ah*).
17. Never make false promises to them.
18. Display equity and justice among them.
19. When the child reaches the age of articulacy, then teach him the correct etiquettes of eating, drinking, laughing, talking, sitting, and walking in accordance with the Prophetic Sunnah. Also, teach the child modesty, respect for elders, reverence for parents, and obedience to teachers. [Girls should be taught to reverence their] husbands.
20. Teach them the Holy Qur'ān. ["Teach them" implies more than mere recitation, it entails thoroughly understanding the actual

---

[71] *Toddlerhood*: One that toddles, especially a young child.
[72] *Adolescence*: The state or process of growing up; the period of life from puberty to maturity.

The Life of a Householder

meaning and spirit of the Book of Allah so that the child may follow its dictums and guidance successfully.]

21. A son should be in the educational care of a teacher who is devote, God-fearing, wise, and experienced.
22. Conversely, daughters should receive instruction from pious female teachers.
23. Qur'ānic recitation must remain constant.
24. Instill in children the correct Islamic beliefs and the importance of the Prophetic Sunnah. Always remember that a clean slate is a natural and willing recipient of the Islamic spirit and open to truth.
25. Plant the seed of love and respect for our Master, the Messenger of Allah ﷺ, firmly in their hearts, as this is the foundation of faith (*Īmān*) and submission (*Islam*).
26. When a child reaches seven years of age, encourage him to perform the ritual prayer (*Salāt*). Teach him the absolute essentials of Islam such as ritual washing (*Wudū*), ritual bathing (*Ghusl*), prayer, and the importance of perseverance, contentment, sincerity, humility, truthfulness, trustworthiness,

justice, modesty, controlling the intellect, and restraining the tongue.

27. Explain to your children the manifest and hidden dangers of heedlessness (*Jahilliya*) like greed, avarice, love of fame and fortune, pride, arrogance, dishonesty, unworthy speech, backbiting, jealousy, and rancor.
28. Employ friendliness and softness when teaching and educating them.
29. Never allow bad companionship for your children.
30. Shield them from speech, looks, and an undesirable environment, because a tender stalk is easy to bend in any direction.
31. It is important to discipline headstrong ten-year-olds that are unwilling to pray.
32. At this age a boy should sleep in his own bed.
33. Children should marry upon reaching maturity.
34. If your children disobey one of your rules, then be affectionate and use tact as a means of mutual consultation.
35. Do not disinherit your children.

36. Be sure to teach boys reading, writing, and guardianship [as the responsibility of providing for the family is upon them].
37. Sūrah al-Mā'idah is very beneficial for boys.

RIGHTS SPECIFIC TO LITTLE WOMEN

38. Do not show displeasure at the birth of a baby girl. In truth, parents should rejoice, because Allah has given them a gift.
39. Girls should learn to sew and cook.
40. Learning Sūrah an-Nūr will be of immense benefit to them.
41. Show greater affection to your daughters than your sons, as their hearts are softer.
42. When giving children anything do not be partial. Be sure to distribute gifts equitably among your sons and daughters.
43. However, daughters should be given their gifts first, and then the boys may receive their gifts in turn.
44. Be attentive to your daughters when they turn nine years of age.
45. They should also sleep in a separate bed at this time.
46. Do not allow them to attend gatherings where music or dancing is present.

Reflections of Allah's Love

47. As a rule, they should not be permitted to interact with strangers.
48. The home is their abode.
49. They should not be allowed on balconies [as this invites unwanted attention, the evil eye (*Nazr*), and leering].
50. Within the home let them adorn themselves with fine clothes and jewelry, so that they may have good proposals for marriage.
51. When their match is found do not delay with the marriage. [Allah the Exalted has said: *Do not prevent them from marrying their husbands.*]⁷³
52. Never marry them to an irreligious person or a sinner, as this is a right in the child's favor established from authentic Ahādīth.

Imām Ahmad ﷺ wraps up his fifty-two points on parenting with these words: "By following these principles a child will become a true embodiment of Islam. Parents must impart these values to their children. At the same time, they should incessantly call on Allah the Exalted so that proper behavior can be actualized. Indeed, Allah Most High has praised those who beseech Him for wives and children in their prayers of supplication (*Du'ā*):

---

⁷³ Al-Qur'ān, 2:232.

The Life of a Householder

And those who say, 'Our Lord, grant us through our wives and children a cooling to the eyes [i.e., solace].'[74] Another Qur'ānic verse instructs the believer to offer this supplication (*Du'ā*): *And correct for me my children, verily I turn to Thee and repent, and verily I am a Muslim.*"[75]

More than anything else, these guidelines emphasize time and again how important it is to love, honor, and cherish one's children and guide them rightly from birth to adulthood. Kind-heartedness toward Muslim children is the central theme of this treatise. Imām Ahmad Razā's advice ؓ on parenting conforms perfectly to the teachings of the Best of Creation ﷺ, and the pious servants of Allah Most High. One of the most celebrated Sufi saints of the Subcontinent, Shaykh Nizām ad-Dīn Awlīyā ؓ (d. 725/1325) in *Morals of the Heart* [Fawa'id al-Fu'ad] corroborates this guidance with the following narrations:

> The Prophet—peace be upon him—had a great affection for children, and liked to frolic with them. "Once," he [Shaykh Nizām ad-Dīn Awlīyā ؓ] noted, "the Prophet—peace be upon him—saw Imam Hasan in a group of children. Coming near,

---

[74] Al-Qur'ān, 25:74.
[75] Al-Qur'ān, 46:15. This slightly modified excerpt was taken from *Islamic Guide for Upbringing Children* which is available from http://thesunniway.com/ebooks/english/category/6-imam-ahmed-rida#, 13.

he put one hand under his chin, the other behind his head and 'kissed his face.'" "They tell a story," I interjected, "about how the Prophet used to play the role of a camel for Hasan and Husayn." "Yes," he rejoined, "this is a famous and well-documented story." On his blessed tongue came this Tradition: "Indeed, here is the camel. (I am) your camel!"

Then he told the following story about the Commander of the Faithful 'Umar—may Allah be pleased with him. "During his Caliphate, he appointed a friend to a high administrative post and had a document drawn up in his name. While the ceremony was taking place, and after he had already presented him the document, the Commander of the Faithful 'Umar—may Allah be pleased with him—took one of his children onto his knee and began playing with him affectionately. That friend looked askance at 'Umar and said: 'I have ten sons. Not one do I cuddle or cajole like this!' Replied 'Umar: 'That document of appointment that I just gave you, give it back to me.' The friend gave it back. 'Umar—may Allah be pleased with him—then tore that document into

The Life of a Householder

shreds, saying 'How can someone who does not care for children show concern for adults?'[76]

Those who try to portray Islam as a cruel religion—obsessed with instilling in children the fear of Allah, the fear of Hell, the fear of death, the fear of sin, and the fear of retribution—have deliberately ignored the teachings of the Holy Qur'ān, the confirmed Hadīth, and the People of Truth (*Ahl al-Haqq*).[77] Muslims and non-Muslims alike should reflect upon these narrations for the Discerner between Truth and Falsehood, 'Umar al-Fārūq ﷺ, was known for his strict adherence to the pure Sharī'ah. He is an archetype of Justice. The author of *Mishalah al-Irshād ila Huquq al-Awlad* was also known to be a strict jurist (*Faqīh*) of the Hanafī school renowned for his scrupulousness. Yet the Commander of the Faithful ﷺ and A'lā Hazrat ﷺ in emulation of the Prophet's ﷺ exemplary way (*Sunnatī*) were gentle, kind, compassionate, and forbearing with

---

[76] Amīr Hasan Sijzi, *Nizām ad-dīn Awliyā: Morals of the Heart* (New Jersey: Paulist Press, 1992), trans. Bruce B. Lawrence, 288-289.

[77] Muslim children should be conscious of Allah. They must be aware of His rights, and our duties unto Him. They should also be taught to remember death, but this must be done in a manner that cultivates love, awe, reverence, and awareness of the Reckoner and the day of reckoning. Instilling awe in the hearts of children ensures that *Taqwā*, virtue, and righteousness prevail at home and in society.

children. 'Umar al-Fārūq ﷺ is an early Muslim (*Salafī*), whilst A'lā Hazrat ﷺ is a latter-day Muslim, and yet there is an undeniable intellectual cohesion and continuity between the two.

Some contemporary Muslims living in the West might shy away from Imām Ahmad Razā's rights specific to little women. But we should refrain from discarding something valuable simply because it fails to conform to our new notions about success in this world (*Dunyā*). In other words, we must not lose sight of the Islamic ideal which is centered on Allah! Each has a goal to which he turns and the life of a Muslim should be dedicated first and foremost to drawing nearer to Allah the Exalted. Men and women were <u>not</u> created to compete with each other in rival careers, but rather they were created to complement one another and serve each other as loving helpmates. On the one hand, a husband is responsible for the welfare of his household, and must spend what he earns to provide for the family. On the other hand, a wife is responsible for safeguarding the sanctity of her husband's home, and must work with his best interest in mind. Each will be questioned on the Day of Judgment about their respective duties. Together they share a common bond, a common commitment, and become one in submission to the Will of Allah like the left and right hand, which come together for *Du'ā*. We often forget that a wife who stays at home is

The Life of a Householder

shielded from the negative influences in society, where passions and malice are increasingly dominant. This is also to her advantage and a source of infinite blessings from the Sublime Lord.

By way of comparison, Western education focuses our daughters' attention on being competitive breadwinners, who abdicate many of their familial roles in order to succeed fiscally. This dubious tunnel vision marginalizes and effectually handicaps their role as a supportive partner, nurturing mother, and conscientious daughter, since it keeps our young women away from their abode. It may be fairly stated that when little women fail to become good wives the larger society suffers at the hands of children, who have grown up dispirited in debased and broken homes. Moreover, secular institutes, as a matter of principle, make absolutely no mention of the next world (*Akhira*). What to speak of raising our daughters with an awareness of life's real purpose.

We now turn our attention to A'lā Hazrat's eldest son, Hāmid Razā Khān ؓ, who became a distinguished scholar-saint of the Qādiriyyah Radawiyyah Tarīqah.⁷⁸ He

---

⁷⁸ *Tarīqah*: Literally "way," as a Sufi order is called, thus the Qādirīyyah Radawīyyah Tarīqah is the "way" of al-Ghawth al-A'zam Sultān al-

was born in the month of Rabī al-Awwal in the year 1292/1875. His venerable father ﷺ personally instructed him in the fields of Hadīth, Islamic jurisprudence (*Fiqh*), and Qur'ānic exegesis (*Tafsīr*). Imām Ahmad Razā ﷺ admired the boy's sincerity and dedication to learning. His love for him was so intense that he would affectionately say: "Hāmid is from me and I am from Hāmid."[79] Indeed there was a striking resemblance between father and son, the latter was a handsome youth with a radiant countenance. This radiance was an outward manifestation of an inward gift, namely, the power of attraction.[80] It has been said that one glance at his noble countenance was enough to turn non-Muslims toward Islam. So manifest was the Light of Sayyidunā Muhammad ﷺ upon the saint's blessed brow that even onlookers would be moved to exclaim, "Here *is* the Proof of Islam (*Hujjat al-Islām*)!"[81]

His smiling countenance was a mark of his inward state of submission and pleasure with the Sunnah of Allah's Messenger ﷺ for it has been narrated by Sayyidah 'Ā'isha ﷺ that she "never saw the noble Prophet ﷺ laugh

---

Awliyā' Sayyidunā ash-Shaykh Muhyi'd-dīn 'Abdul Qādir al-Jīlānī al-Hasanī al-Husainī ﷺ and Imām al-Akbar Shaykh al-Islam wal-Muslimīn 'Ārife-Billāh A'lā Hazrat Mujaddid Imām Ahmad Razā Khān al-Qādirī al-Barkātī ﷺ.

[79] Mawlānā Muhammad Afthab Cassim, *The Chain of Light*, 2:121.
[80] Cf. "The State of Excellence: An Explanation of Islam and Sufism," accessed on October 2, 2011, http://naqshbandi.org/about/aexplain.htm.
[81] Mawlānā Muhammad Afthab Cassim, *The Chain of Light*, 2:122.

The Life of a Householder

so much that the palate of his (blessed) mouth could be seen. He only smiled."[82] Kharijah bin Zayd ؓ also said that the Prophet's laughter was "no more than a smile" and that the Companions' laughter in his esteemed presence was smiling too.[83] Shaykh Hāmid Razā Khān's ؓ speech was measured, calm, and dignified. He had tremendous regard for elders, and immense love for children. He made it a point to lower his gaze when conversing or walking in the street, and he always chose to dress in simple attire.[84] At the age of nineteen, he graduated with distinction from Dār al-'Ulūm Manzar al-Islām in Bareilly, India.

Most of his spare time was spent reciting *Salawāt*.[85] His body and soul were so engrossed in *Salawāt* that he continued to audibly send blessings upon the Prophet ﷺ in his sleep![86] How perfectly he fulfilled the words of our Lord: *Verily, Allah and His Angels send blessings upon the Prophet. O you who believe! Send blessings on him and salute him with a worthy salutation.*[87] Al-Bukhārī ؓ narrates from Jābir ibn 'Abdullāh ؓ that the angels came to the Prophet

---

[82] Muftī Jalāl ad-Dīn Ahmad al-Qādirī al-Amjadī, *In Light of the Sacred Traditions of the Beloved* ﷺ, 398.
[83] See Qādī 'Iyād's *ash-Shifā*, 1:107.
[84] Mawlānā Muhammad Afthab Cassim, *The Chain of Light*, 2:122-123.
[85] *Salawāt*: Prayers, blessings, and benedictions upon our Master, Prophet Muhammad ﷺ.
[86] Mawlānā Muhammad Afthab Cassim, *The Chain of Light*, 2:122.
[87] Al-Qur'ān, 33:56.

Reflections of Allah's Love

ﷺ while he was asleep. One of them said, "He is asleep." Another of them said, "The eye is asleep but the heart is awake." They said [by way of making an example of this comparison], "The house is the Garden and one who invites people is Muhammad ﷺ. Whoever obeys Muhammad ﷺ has obeyed Allah. Whoever disobeys Muhammad ﷺ has disobeyed Allah. Muhammad differentiates between the people."[88] Sayyidah 'Ā'isha ؓ once asked the Messenger of Allah ﷺ, "Do you sleep before *witr*?" He answered her, "'**Ā'isha, my eyes sleep but my heart does not sleep.**"[89]

The eyes of the elite (*Khāss*) sleep, but their hearts are always enlivened with the remembrance (*Dhikr*) of Allah and His Messenger ﷺ. It is narrated that at the time of death, Sayyid Shāh Āl-e Rasūl ؓ (the Grand Shaykh of Hujjat al-Islām ؓ) continued to recite *Dhikr*, even though his physical heart had stopped beating! His saintly grandson and *Sajjād Nashin*,[90] Sayyid Shāh Abu'l Husain Ahmad an-Nūrī Marehrawī ؓ, appealed to the soul (*Rūh*) of Shāh Āl-e Rasūl ؓ beseeching him to stop moving his

---

[88] Al-Bukhārī ؓ in his *Sahīh*, "The Book of Holding Fast to the Book and the Sunna," trans. Ustādha Āisha Bewley, accessed on December 8, 2011, http://spl.qibla.com/Hadith/H0002P0099.aspx.
[89] Al-Bukhārī ؓ in his *Sahīh*, "The Book of Tahajjud Prayers," trans. Ustādha Āisha Bewley, accessed on December 8, 2011, http://spl.qibla.com/Hadith/H0002P0025.aspx.
[90] *Sajjād Nashin*: One of the foremost deputies of a Murshid and the keeper of his Sufi center (*Khānqah*).

The Life of a Householder

lips since those gathered for his funeral would no doubt become disquieted at the sight of this miraculous event (*Karāmāt*). Shāh Āl-e Rasūl's soul ﷺ acquiesced to his grandson's request after the third appeal.[91]

Allah the Exalted has said: *And say not of those who are slain (martyred) in the Way of Allah, "they are dead." Nay, they are living, though you perceive it not!*[92] And: *They (martyrs) are alive in the presence of their Lord, being provided for.*[93] The People of the Sunnah have confirmed that what is true of martyrs in the aforementioned verses is true of the Prophets, of the Sufi saints, and of the righteous Muslims as well. They are alive. This belief is firmly established through authentic and explicit proofs.

Shaykh Hāmid Razā ﷺ was conferred numerous titles by the *Ahl al-Sunnah wa al-Jamā'ah*, such as "The Leader of the Islamic Scholars" (*Raīs al-'Ulamā*), "The Crown of Righteousness" (*Tāj al-Atqiyā*), "The Shaykh of the Hadīth Masters" (*Shaykh al-Muhadithīn*), and most notably "The Proof of Islam" (*Hujjat al-Islām*).[94] One of these dignitaries, Shaykh Dya' ad-Dīn Madanī[95] ﷺ who was famously

---

[91] Sayyid Abu'l Husain Ahmad an-Nūrī, *Horizons of Perfection* (Durban: Barkātur-Razā Publications, 2005), trans. Shaykh 'Abdul Hādī, 52-53.
[92] Al-Qur'ān, 2:154.
[93] Al-Qur'ān, 3: 169.
[94] Mawlānā Muhammad Afthab Cassim, *The Chain of Light*, 2:121.
[95] *Madanī*: A surname ending in –ī will often indicate the bearer's place of birth. Shaykh Dya' ad-Dīn was born in the illumined city of Medina.

recognized as the Lordly Cardinal Pole (*Qutb*) of Medina, observed: "Hujjat al-Islām was a brilliant personality and a handsome youth. He was an incredibly humble person. Whenever I journeyed from Medina the Illumined to Bareilly Sharīf, he was an exemplary host. He would personally shine my shoes with his own cloth. He never permitted anyone to serve me, and singlehandedly served *all* my meals to me. It is difficult to express the extent of his hospitality. When I would prepare to return to the illumined city of Medina, he would humbly say: 'Please convey my salutations in the exalted Court of our Master, the Messenger of Allah ﷺ, and pray that he invites me to the Holy City.'"[96]

On the Night of Absolution (*Lailat al-Barā'a*) he would entreat those around him to forgive him his trespasses against them. Children, servants, and disciples were not to be excluded from his petitions for forgiveness. On the 15th of Sha'bān, he would always say, "If I have been the cause of any pain to you, then please forgive me. If I owe anything to anyone, then please let me know."[97] This is a classic example of God-fear (*Taqwā*), for our Prophet ﷺ said: **"When the night of mid-Sha'bān arrives, Allah makes careful scrutiny of His creatures, then He forgives the true believers, gives respite to the unbelievers, and**

---

[96] Mawlānā Muhammad Afthab Cassim, *The Chain of Light*, 2:123.
[97] Ibid., 2:124.

The Life of a Householder

leaves the resentful to their resentment until they call for Him."[98] He also said: **"One who [sincerely] repents from sin is like one who has not sinned."**[99] There is another noble utterance (*Hadīth Sharīf*) that gives a positive command to forgive the one who asks for forgiveness, and accept his apology. If a Muslim refuses to forgive his brother, then he will not be permitted to drink from the Prophet's ﷺ Lake-Fount (*Kauthar*) in Paradise.[100] From this one anecdote we learn the importance of humility, asking forgiveness from others for the offences we knowingly and unknowingly commit, and the significance of accepting our brother's apology with all our heart.

Allah willing, we will return to the personal narrative of Shaykh Hāmid Razā ﷺ in the forthcoming chapters.

---

[98] Shaykh 'Abdul Qādir al-Jīlānī, *Sufficient Provision for Seekers of the Path of Truth* (Hollywood: Al-Baz Publishing, Inc., 1997), trans. Muhtar Holland, 3:67.

[99] This noble utterance is cited by Ibn Mājah in his *Sunan* and at-Tabarānī in his *al-Mu'jam al-Kabīr*. Also see, Imām Ahmad Razā Khān, "Muslim Rights" in *Thesis of Imam Ahmad Raza* (Durban: Barkātur-Razā Publications, 2005), trans. Shaykh 'Abdul Hādī, 3:71.

[100] Imām Ahmad Razā Khān, *Luminous Glad-tidings Pertaining to the Laws of Hajj and Ziyārah* (Durban: Imam Mustafa Raza Research Centre, 2011), trans. Mawlānā Muhammad Afthab Cassim, 2.

The Abode of Great Saints

In 1878, Mawlānā 'Abdul Qādir Badayunī ؓ invited 'Allāma Naqī ؓ and Imām Ahmad Razā ؓ to meet the Barkātiyya Sayyids of Marehra Sharīf. Both father and son were looking forward to undertaking this pilgrimage (*Ziyārat*), since the rector of the Sufi center in Marehra (*Khānqah*), Sayyid Shāh Āl-e Rasūl ؓ (d. 1296/1879), was a descendant of the Messenger of Allah ﷺ through his grandson Imām Husain ؓ. He was widely recognized by the elite in his time to be the Lordly Cardinal Pole of the Era (*Qutb al-Waqt*) and the Seal of the Dignitaries (*Khātim al-Akābir*). His righteous ancestors migrated from the illumined city of Medina to Iraq, because of political persecution. Later the family moved to the Subcontinent where they finally settled in Marehra in accordance with the divine decree. His genealogy can be traced through a prestigious line of scholar-saints, who devoted themselves assiduously to spiritual realization, and a life of worshipful service (*'Ibādah*) and spiritual retreat (*I`tikāf*).

The Abode of Great Saints

To this day Marehra remains a center of pilgrimage and reverence in the Subcontinent.

Sayyid Shāh Āl-e Rasūl ؓ is the son of Shāms ad-Dīn[101] Abu'l Fadhl[102] Sayyid Shāh Āl-e Ahmad "Acchey Miya" ؓ (d. 1235/1820), who is the son of Qutb al-Kāmilīn[103] Sayyid Shāh Hamza ؓ (d. 1198/1783), who is the son of Abu'l-Barakāt[104] Sayyid Shāh Āl-e Muhammad ؓ (d. 1164/1751), who is the son of Sayyid al-Mutakalimīn[105] Sultān al-Āshiqīn[106] Sayyid Shāh Barkatu'llāh ؓ (d. 1070/1729) of Marehra Sharīf.

The blessed mausoleum (*Dargāh*) of the Barkātiyya Sayyids in Marehra Sharīf.

Sayyid Shāh Āl-e Rasūl's father (Hazrat Acchey Miya ؓ) was a renowned Gnostic (*'Ārif*) and many a wayfarer (*Sālik*) flocked his court for guidance concerning spiritual matters. Once, Shāh 'Abdul 'Azīz ؓ, the celebrated

---

[101] *Shāms ad-Dīn*: "The Sun of the Faith."
[102] *Abu'l Fadhl*: "The Father of Grace."
[103] *Qutb al-Kāmilīn*: "The Lordly Cardinal Pole of Perfection."
[104] *Abu'l Barakāt*: "The Father of Blessings."
[105] *Sayyid al-Mutakalimīn*: "The Leader of the Scholastic Theologians."
[106] *Sultān al-Āshiqīn*: "The Sultān of the Lovers."

Reflections of Allah's Love

Muhadīth of Delhi, sent one such *sālik* to him. This seeker of knowledge had been troubled by a particularly esoteric question regarding Divine Oneness, and in his search for an answer had travelled far and long. In his travels he had visited the chief noblemen (*Naqīb al-Ashrāf*) of Iraq before visiting Delhi, and from Delhi had found his way at last to Marehra. It was in Marehra at the hands of Sayyid Acchey Miya he at last received the illumination that he sought, and his burning question was finally answered, as Shāh 'Abdul 'Azīz ؓ expected.[107]

Sayyid Acchey Miya's father (Sayyid Shāh Hamza ؓ) had similarly achieved a high state of spirituality. A special gift that he was blessed with was the vision (*Rūyā*) of Allah's Messenger ﷺ whenever he recited certain *Salawāt*. He not only beheld the Beloved of the Lord of all the worlds ﷺ in his dreams, but also with his waking eyes! He also beheld the ennobled face of 'Alī ibn Abī Tālib ؓ holding the pillars of the Khānqah, as well. During the vision, the fourth Caliph ؓ assured Sayyid Shāh Hamza: "You are my son, and my beloved descendent."[108]

Sayyid Shāh Hamza's father (Sayyid Shāh Āl-e Muhammad ؓ) spent his whole life in the company of the Friends of Allah, and was one of those who shun the world (*Zāhid*). He devoted three years to continuous

---

[107] Mawlānā Muhammad Afthab Cassim, *The Chain of Light*, 2:73.
[108] Ibid., 2:70.

The Abode of Great Saints

spiritual retreat (*I`tikāf*), fasting incessantly, and only opening his fast with dry bread and a few drops of water.[109]

Sayyid Shāh Āl-e Muhammad's father (Sayyid Shāh Barkatu'llāh) ؉ was a true ascetic of this world that lived by the Word of Allah alone. He fasted continuously for twenty-six years, and opened his fast with a single date. This decided proclivity towards asceticism was clearly indicative of a very high station in spirituality (*Rūhāniyya*). For three years he subsisted merely on water strained from rice and would remain in ecstasy (*Hal*) for weeks on end.[110] Following the command he received in a dream (*Bashārat*) from Allah's Messenger ؉ and Sayyidunā ash-Shaykh 'Abdul Qādir al-Jīlānī ؉ he decided to settle in Marehra.[111] Here he established a Sufi center that came to be known as the Abode of Great Saints (*Bastī Pīrzadagan*).

Considering the spiritual stature of his perfected guide (*Murshid al-Kāmil*), it should come as no surprise that A'lā Hazrat ؉ immediately perceived the fragrant scent of Sayyid Shāh Āl-e Rasūl ؉, upon reaching the terminal in

---

[109] Mawlānā Muhammad Afthab Cassim, *The Chain of Light*, 2:66.
[110] Ibid., 2:57.
[111] Ibid., 2:58.

Marehra. The secret of this reality is mentioned in a famous couplet by Kabīr ﷺ:

Fragrance of the flower spreads
  Its sweetness in the air
None can see and catch it though
  You find it in the saint and seer.[112]

After inviting the guests from Bareilly into the Khānqah, Sayyid Shāh Āl-e Rasūl ﷺ enigmatically said to the young Imām ﷺ, "I have been awaiting your presence for a long time."[113] As is the wont of the Sufis, in accordance with the Prophetic Sunnah, Imām Ahmad Razā ﷺ swore an oath of allegiance (*Bayah*) to Sayyid Shāh Āl-e Rasūl ﷺ who, in turn, announced that the young Imām was his deputy (*Khalīfah*) and gave him permission to transmit knowledge (*Ijāzat*) in every line (*Silsilat*) of Sufism (*Tasawwuf*).[114]

There was a procedure at Marehra Sharīf by which a disciple (*Murīd*) had to undergo rigorous spiritual practice

---

[112] G.N. Das, *Couplets from Kabir* (Delhi: Motilal Banarsidass Publications, 1999), 30.
[113] Mawlānā Muhammad Afthab Cassim, *Imam Ahmad Raza*, 55.
[114] *Silsilat*: The initiatic genealogy or chain: each Master's authority derived from that of his predecessor who, in turn, was linked to another predecessor, going back in a chain to the first Sufi, in all but name, the Prophet himself ﷺ.

The Abode of Great Saints

(*Mujāhidah*) and subsist on dried bread. If he completed this training, then he was given a license (*Ijāzat*) to teach others and entrusted with lieutenancy (*Khilāfat*). By blessing this young guest from Bareilly, with everything the seeker longs for, it probably seemed to most of the onlookers that Sayyid Shāh Āl-e Rasūl ﷺ broke a family tradition! Hence, Shāh Abu'l Husain Ahmad ﷺ (also known as Nūrī Miyān) asked their Murshid al-Kāmil for an explanation: Why was this young man blessed with *Khalīfah* and *Ijāzat* in all the *Silsilat*, and even commanded to look at and verify all of their Murshid's books? Being a profound Gnostic, Sayyid Shāh Abu'l Husain ﷺ already knew the answer to his question. But he made the enquiry for the group's *esprit de corps* and spiritual edification.[115]

Thus spoke their illustrious Sufi Shaykh, "O People! You do not know Ahmad Razā. Others who come here need to be prepared before gaining *Ijāzat* and *Khilāfat*. But Ahmad Razā Khān has come prepared from Allah the Exalted. All he needed was a link and this is why I made him my *murīd*." He continued, "For years I've cried out in fear of Allah, because on the Day of Judgment, if He were to question me concerning what I had brought Him from this world, then I would have no answer. But today that fear no longer exists. If on the Day of Judgment the Almighty asks, 'O Āl-e Rasūl, what have you brought for

---

[115] Mawlānā Muhammad Afthab Cassim, *Imam Ahmad Raza*, 56.

Me?' Then I will readily present Imām Ahmad Razā Khān to my Creator."¹¹⁶ Such was the spiritual prowess of this matchless personality who, despite his uniquely endowed station and rank, remained an ardent devotee of his Master ﷺ and a humble servant of the Barkātiyya Sayyids.

This is evidenced by the fact that whenever Imām Ahmad Razā ؓ went to Marehra Sharīf to visit his beloved Murshid al-Kāmil ؓ he would remove his shoes at the railway station and walk barefoot to the Khānqah. Similarly whenever a representative from Marehra Sharīf came to Bareilly, the Imām would show his distinguished guest great deference. He would greet the representative with the utmost courtesy (*Ādāb*) and personally ensured that he partook of a sumptuous meal. As a mark of humility and respect, Imām Ahmad Razā ؓ would carry the meal upon his head.¹¹⁷

Prior to his union (*Wisāl*), Sayyid Shāh Āl-e Rasul ؓ made his grandson (Sayyid Shāh Abu'l Husain Ahmad ؓ) the keeper of the Khānqah (*Sajjād Nashin*). Hazrat Nūrī Miyān had reached the peak of spiritual excellence (*Ihsān*) in his adolescent years.¹¹⁸ He was considered by many to be the Pole Star of Marehra (*Qutb al-Irshād*) and the Lamp

---

¹¹⁶ Mawlānā Muhammad Afthab Cassim, *Imam Ahmad Raza*, 55-56.
¹¹⁷ Ibid., 57.
¹¹⁸ Sayyid Shāh Abu'l Husain Ahmad, *Horizons of Perfection*, x.

The Abode of Great Saints

of the Gnostics (*Sirāj al-'Ārifīn*).[119] He derived a profuse amount of grace (*Fuyūd*) and divine blessings (*Barakāt*) from the *Mashā'ikh* of Marehra, Bilgram, and Murādabād. His teachers in the field of Islamic spirituality (*Tasawwuf*) included:

- Khātim al-Akābir Sayyid Shāh Āl-e Rasul ⚘,
- Tāj al-'Ārifīn Sayyid Shāh Ghūlām Muhyi'd-dīn Amīr al-'Ālam,
- Shaykh Sayyid 'Ayn al-Hasan Bilgrāmī, and
- Shaykh Ahmad Husan Sufi Murādabādī.

He also met with the Prophets and Sufi saints, who continue to guide the Community in their isthmus-life (*al-Hayāt al-Barzakhiyya*) between death and Resurrection, as Allah the Exalted says: *They live, finding their sustenance in the presence of their Lord.*[120] Hazrat Nūrī Miyān ⚘ met with the following Prophets and Sufi saints through mystical gifts and powers of vision:[121]

---

[119] *Sirāj* is an Arabic word meaning: (1) to shine, to be bright, (2) a lamp or candle, (3) the sun. This is a very profound title as it informs us that Shāh Abu'l Husain Ahmad ⚘ is the Sun of the day and the Lamp that shines upon the Gnostics at night.

[120] Al-Qur'ān, 3:169.

[121] To receive such knowledge is a gift (*Karāmāt*) for the saint, and the process of receiving it is known as inspiration (*Ilham*), or vision (*Rūyā*), unveiling (*Kashf*), piercing sight (*Firasa*), or glad tidings (*Mubashshira*)

- The Master of the Messengers ﷺ, with whom he embraced and shook hands. He then had the extraordinary honor of taking *Bayah*, and the privilege of sitting beside the Messenger of Allah ﷺ during his sanctified assemblies (*Majlis*).
- Our Master, Prophet Mūsā ؑ.
- Our Master, Prophet Sulaymān ؑ.
- Our Master, Prophet 'Īsā ibn Maryam ؑ.
- Our Master, 'Alī ibn Abī Tālib ؓ.
- Our Master, Imām Husain ؓ.
- Al-Ghawth al-A'zam Sultān al-Awliyā' Sayyidunā ash-Shaykh Muhyi'd-dīn 'Abdul Qādir al-Jīlānī al-Hasanī al-Husainī ؓ.
- The Master of the Masters, Khawaja Muīn ad-Dīn Hasan Gharīb Nawāz ؓ.
- Our Master, Shaykh Zun-Nūn al-Misrī ؓ.
- Our Master, Khawaja 'Uthmān Hir'wanī ؓ.
- The Gnostic Superior, our Master, Mīr Khawaja 'Abdul Jalīl al-Husainī Chishtī ؓ.

---

from Allah, disclosure (*Mukashafa*), mutual vision (*Mushahada*), or divine conversation (*Mukhataba*).

- And his entire family of *Mashā'ikh* that preceded him in death, may Allah be well-pleased with them.[122]

Hazrat Nūrī Miyān ﷺ was blessed with an impeccable personality. It was his wont to exchange his clothes with indigents by expressing his sincere desire to possess their tattered garments. This, of course, made the impoverished person very happy. After receiving these worn clothes, he would hasten to his home and present a gift of new clothes to the individual as a token of his appreciation. He slept no more than four hours a day, and spent most of his time engrossed in Sufi meditation (*Murāqabah*). He was also the last of the senior *Mashā'ikh* of the noble Barkātiyya Sayyids to regularly engage in the Inverted Prayer (*Salāt al-Ma'kūs*), which is a specialty of those following the Chishtī order. The devotee suspends himself upside down in a well with a rope tied around his ankles and preforms this mystical prayer from midnight until the arrival of the Night Vigil Prayer (*Salāt at-Tahajjud*), just before true dawn (*Subhu-Sādiq*). As a result of performing this divinely inspired prayer, there was a black ring around his blessed ankles. Yet he never missed a single Tahajjud prayer, and reaped the paradisiacal rewards of one of the most praiseworthy supererogatory acts of devotion. He

---

[122] Sayyid Shāh Abu'l Husain Ahmad, *Horizons of Perfection*, xix-xx.

began to perform this prayer when he was only six years old.[123]

Sayyid Shāh Āl-e Rasūl ﷺ chose his *Sajjād Nashin* well, for his grandson ﷺ was a living example of extinction in the Shaykh (*Fanā fi'l Shaykh*). Ghūlām Shabbar Qādirī Nūrī Badayunī in his *Tazkira-e Nūrī: Mufassal Halat o Sawanih-e Abu'l Husain Nūrī Miyān* records how this remarkable Sufi saint was the epitome of death before dying (*Fanā*):

"[Nūrī Miyān ﷺ] loved and respected his [Pīr, Shāh Āl-e Rasūl ﷺ]; indeed, he loved everyone who was associated with him, and all the members of his family. He followed his commands, he presented himself before him at his court (*darbar*), he sought his company, he was completely absorbed in him. His face had the same radiance [as Shāh Āl-e Rasūl ﷺ], his personality had the same stamp (*hal*), he walked with the same gait, when he talked it was in the same tone. His clothes had the same appearance; he dealt with others in the same way. In his devotions and strivings, he followed the same path (*maslak*). The times set apart for rest in the afternoon and sleep at night were times when he went to him particularly, receiving from him

---

[123] Sayyid Shāh Abu'l Husain Ahmad, *Horizons of Perfection*, xxiii.

The Abode of Great Saints

guidance in every matter and warning of every danger. (Ghūlām Shabbar Qādirī, 1968: 91)"[124]

Before closing this chapter, it is worth noting that Hazrat Nūrī Miyān ⚜ taught Imām Ahmad Razā ⚜ the Art of Divination (*'Ilm al-Jafr*).[125] Not only was he one of A'lā Hazrat's distinguished teachers, but his brother in Tarīqah (*Pīr bhai*) too. He guided the young Imām's steps and declared him to be "a radiantly shining lamp from the house of divine blessings (*Khāndan al-Barakāt*)."[126] Although their Murshid al-Kāmil ⚜ forsook this ephemeral world in 1879, his foremost disciples and deputies enjoyed an everlasting spiritual bond with him. Indeed, the bond of friendship that developed between his *Sajjād Nashin* ⚜ and the *Mujaddid* of Bareilly ⚜ proved to be an unbreakable golden chain (*Silsilat*) that bears their names to this day.[127]

---

[124] Sanyal, *Ahmad Riza Khan Barelwi*, 91.
[125] Imām Mustafā Razā Khān, *al-Malfūz al-Sharīf*, 2:200.
[126] Mawlānā Muhammad Afthab Cassim, *Imam Ahmad Raza*, 104.
[127] At-Tarīqat al-'Ālīyat al-Qādirīyat al-Barakātīyat al-Radawīyat an-Nūrīyah.

Journey to the Holy House

In 1295/1878, Imām Ahmad Razā ﷺ undertook the Pilgrimage (*Hajj*) to Mecca the Ennobled with his esteemed parents. Here he received recognition and training from Shaykh Husain Sālih ﷺ (the Imām of the Shāfi'ī school), Shaykh Abdur Rahmān al-Sirāj ﷺ (the Muftī of the Hanafī school), and Shaykh ash-Sayyid Ahmad ibn Zayni Dahlan ﷺ (the Muftī of the Shāfi'ī school and Chief Justice[128] of Mecca). Shaykh ash-Sayyid Ahmad ibn Zayni Dahlan ﷺ and Shaykh Abdur Rahman al-Sirāj ﷺ gave him a certificate (*Sanad*) in several fields of knowledge including Hadīth, Qur'ānic exegesis (*Tafsīr*), applied jurisprudence (*Fiqh*), and the principles of jurisprudence (*Usūl al-Fiqh*).[129] At the age of twenty-three, Imām Ahmad Razā ﷺ had mastered both the Hanafī and Shāfi'ī schools of Sunni law.

Shaykh Husain Sālih ash-Shāfi'ī ﷺ saw Allah's light shining radiantly upon the Imām's blessed brow and took

---

[128] *Qādī al-Qudāt* is an Arabic appellation for the Chief Justice of the Sharī'ah courts. This is the highest post an Islamic judge can attain.
[129] Sanyal, *Ahmad Riza Khan Barelwi*, 63-64.

Journey to the Holy House

this remarkable youth aside after reading the evening prayer. He then conferred upon him the title *Zia ad-Dīn* (or, "The Glory of the Religion"). And blessed him with certificates of authorization (*Sanad*) in the six great collections of Hadīth (*Sihāh al-Sittah*),[130] as well as one in the Qādirī Tarīqah signing it with his own hand.[131]

From Mecca the Ennobled, Imām Ahmad Razā ﷺ traveled to Medina the Illumined to pay a visit (*Ziyārat*) to Allah's Beloved ﷺ. Sunnis have always engaged in this meritorious practice in accordance with the Prophetic Hadīth. For it is our belief that the Prophets, saints, martyrs, and righteous Muslims are alive in their graves, and that they are a means (*Wasīla*) for gaining the blessings and forgiveness of Allah Most Pure. Abū Hurayrah ﷺ reports on the authority of Ahmad ﷺ and Abū Dāwūd ﷺ that Allah's Messenger ﷺ said: **"None of you greets me except that Allah returns my soul unto me and I return his greeting."**[132] Anas ibn Mālik ﷺ narrates that the Messenger of Allah ﷺ said: **"The Prophets are alive in their grave performing the ritual prayer**

---

[130] *Sihāh al-Sittah* refers to the rigorously-authenticated (*Sahīh*) compilations of al-Bukhārī ﷺ, Muslim ﷺ, Ibn Mājah ﷺ, Abū Dāwūd ﷺ, at-Tirmidhī ﷺ and an-Nasā'ī ﷺ.
[131] Sanyal, *Ahmad Riza Khan Barelwi*, 63-64.
[132] Narrated by Ahmad ﷺ and Abū Dāwūd ﷺ.

(Salāt)."[133] Aws ibn Aws al-Thaqafī ﷺ narrated on the authority of Abū Dāwūd ﷺ, an-Nasā'ī ﷺ, Ibn Mājah ﷺ, Ahmad ﷺ, and others (all with a sound chain meeting Muslim's criterion ﷺ) that the Prophet ﷺ ordered us to send salutations upon him in abundance on Friday, as our salutations are presented to him. The Companions inquired: "How will it be possible for you to receive our salutations when your mortal frame has been laid to rest?" The Prophet ﷺ replied: **"Allah, the Exalted, has forbidden the earth from consuming the bodies of the Prophets!"**[134]

For a true Lover of the Messenger ﷺ (*Āshiq al-Rasūl*), there is no greater pleasure or honor in this life than visiting the blessed mausoleum of the Chosen One ﷺ with whom Allah is well pleased. This ardent love has been immortalized in A'lā Hazrat's famous couplet:

O Pilgrims! Come to the mausoleum of the king of kings
You have seen the Ka'ba, now see the Ka'ba of the Ka'ba

Although Hāmid Razā ﷺ was but a wee baby in his mother's lap, he would one day become a great poet himself, who shared his father's ardor:

---

[133] This Hadīth Sharīf is recorded by al-Bayhaqī in his *Hayāt al-Anbiya'* [The Life of the Prophets] and Abū Ya'lā al-Mawsilī in his *Musnad*.
[134] Aws ibn Aws al-Thaqafī ﷺ narrated this Hadīth Sharīf on the authority of Abū Dāwūd, an-Nasā'ī, Ibn Mājah, Ahmad, and others.

Journey to the Holy House

O Beloved! Call us to Medina now. Let us behold your Green Dome. Your servants in India, Hāmid and Mustafā,[135] are longing to meet you.

Imām Ahmad Razā ؓ authored a guidebook on Hajj and visitation entitled *Anwār al-Bashārah fi Masā'ilī Hajj wal Ziyārat* [Luminous Glad Tidings Pertaining to the Laws of Hajj and Visitation]. His father's book *Jawāhir al-Bayān Sharīf* [The Unveiling of Precious Gems] forms the basis of this work, and sheds light on the protocol they observed whilst visiting the illumined city of Medina. Some choice points from this wonderful book, which has recently been translated into English by Mawlānā Muhammad Afthab Cassim, are being presented here for the benefit of the reader:

1. To be present (*Hāzirī*) in the sanctified Court of the noble Prophet ﷺ is near *Wājib* [in the Hanafī school].[136] Some people will act as though they are your well-wishers and try to dissuade you from

---

[135] Mustafā Razā Khān ؓ is A'lā Hazrat's younger son (b. 1310/1892).
[136] *Wājib:* Necessary. Leaving a *Wājib* action entails punishment like something obligatory (*Fard*), and its performance entails reward like the *Fard*. However, denying its necessary nature does not entail disbelief like the *Fard*.

visiting the Prophet ﷺ in Medina the Illumined. They will say there is danger along the way and an epidemic there. Be wary! Do not listen to their insidious tales, and deprive yourself from visiting the illumined city of Medina, thus marring your Pilgrimage (*Hajj*) with an unsightly blemish. Since one has to die sooner than later, why not die while travelling to the Holy Prophet ﷺ. I know from direct experience that if you cling to the skirt (*Dāman*) of the Prophet ﷺ, then you will come under his protection and he will guide you and shield you from all calamities.[137]

2. When visiting Medina make a special intention to visit the Prophet ﷺ. Imām Ibn Humām ؓ, the famous Hanafī Mujtāhid, has said: "On this occasion, do not even make the intention of visiting the Mosque (but make the intention of visiting the Prophet ﷺ)."

3. Throughout the journey engross yourself in the recitation of *Salawāt* and divine remembrance (*Dhikr*).

4. Once the Sanctuary (*Haram*) of Medina is visible, it is better to travel on foot. Walk towards the

---

[137] A'lā Hazrat ؓ wrote this book in 1329/1911 after he had successfully performed an obligatory (1295/1878) and a supererogatory (1323/1905) Pilgrimage.

Haram crying with your head bowed and gaze lowered. If possible do so barefoot.
5. Send blessings and salutations in abundance as soon as you can see the Green Dome of the Prophet's blessed mausoleum ﷺ.
6. When you reach the blessed city of Medina drown yourself in the thought of the majesty (*Jalāl*), and beauty (*Jamāl*) of the Beloved Prophet ﷺ.
7. To be present (*Hāzirī*) in the Mosque of the Prophet ﷺ (*Masjid an-Nabī* ﷺ), you must clear your heart of all thoughts and relieve yourself of all needs that may disturb you. Be sure to avoid unnecessary conversation too. Perform the ritual ablution (*Wudū'*) immediately and use the toothstick (*Miswāk*). To perform the major ablution (*Ghusal*) is more virtuous than *Wudū'*. It is preferable to wear clean, white clothing. If you have the means then wear new clothes. Apply fragrance and kohl. Musk is the preferred fragrance.
8. Turn towards the Sacred Tomb (*Rauza al-Aqdas*) with ample love and reverence. If your eyes do not overflow with tears then look sad. Beseech the Messenger of Allah ﷺ to break your heart of stone, and induce it to weep.

Reflections of Allah's Love

9. At the entrance of the Mosque send blessings and salutations upon the Prophet ﷺ. Then wait at the door and seek permission to enter from the Master (*Sarkār*) of the House ﷺ. You must invoke the Name of Allah [by saying "*Bismi'llāh*"], and enter with the right foot in a state of reverence and awe.

10. Your heart knows the protocol and veneration [due to the Prophet ﷺ], which is incumbent upon every Muslim in this moment. The bodily organs should be free from all other thoughts and desires. Do not be engrossed in the calligraphy or inscriptions on the Mosque. (All of your attention should be on the Messenger of Allah ﷺ.)

11. Only speak according to necessity, even when someone comes before you with the intention to converse. Do not engage in idle conversation. With all your heart establish a link to the Prophet ﷺ.

12. Never raise your voice or shout at anything or anyone in the Sacred Mosque.

13. Believe with earnest conviction that the Holy Prophet ﷺ is alive and present (*Hādir*) just as he was before passing from this world (*Dunyā*). All the Prophets (peace be upon them) taste death only for a fraction of a second to fulfill the

promise of Allah the Exalted. Their passing between the states of life and death concealed them from us, but we are not concealed from them. 'Allāma Ahmad Qastallānī ﷺ has stated in his book *al-Mawāhib al-Ladunnīya* as did Imām Muhammad ibn Hajar al-Makkī ﷺ in his *Madkhal* that: "There is no difference between the states of life and death of the Prophet ﷺ, as he sees his entire Umma and recognizes their states, their intentions, and their minds, and all this is clear to him, there is no secret thereof to him." Imām Rahmatu'llāh ﷺ, the student of Imām Ibn Humām ﷺ, in his *al-Mansak al-Mutawasit* and Mullā 'Alī al-Qārī al-Makkī ﷺ in his *Mirqāt al-Mafātīh sharh Mishkāt al-Masābīh* have said: "Verily, the Messenger of Allah ﷺ is aware of your presence, your standing, your salutation, all of your actions, and your doings and position."

14. If the congregational prayer is already in progress then join it, as this will fulfill the Prayer of Greeting the Mosque (*Tahīyat al-Masjid*). If you missed the congregational prayer, then still offer two cycles of *Tahīyat al-Masjid* as an expression of gratitude (*Shukrāna*) for being present in Masjid an-Nabī ﷺ! Read Sūrah 109: al-Kāfirūn [The Unbelievers] in the first cycle, and Sūrah 112: al-

Ikhlās [Sincere Devotion] in the second. Try to pray at the place where the Messenger of Allah ﷺ performed his ritual prayers. If you cannot obtain this [coveted] site then try to say your prayers as close to it as possible. After offering this prayer, perform the prostration of thankfulness (*Sajdah as-Shukr*) and offer the following supplication (*Du'ā*): "O Allah! Give us the opportunity to truly venerate Your Beloved ﷺ. Bless us with Your approval and his acceptance, Āmīn."

15. Bow your head and lower your gaze with the utmost spiritual courtesy (*Ādāb*), trembling from the fear of Allah, perspiring due to the shame of your sins. Place your faith and hope in the mercy and blessing of the Prophet ﷺ. You should approach Allah's Messenger ﷺ from the eastern vicinity of the Masjid and stand at his feet with your back to the Ka'ba for the Prophet's ﷺ luminous Tomb (*Mazār al-Anwār*) is facing the Qibla. Enter from this direction so that the sight of the Prophet ﷺ may be upon you, and this is sufficient for you in both the worlds.

16. With reverence, fear, and hope stand under the chandelier close to the silver peg embedded in the southern door of the chamber of purification (*Hujra al-Mutāhira*), and face the blessed

countenance of the Messenger of Allah ﷺ. Stand at least four hand lengths away with your back to the *Qibla*, directly facing the luminous Tomb (*Mazār al-Anwār*), and place your right hand upon the left hand below the navel, as in prayer. This practice has been recommended in *al-Lubāb fī Sharh al-Kitāb* by Shaykh 'Abdul Ghanī al-Maydanī ؒ (who was a student of Ibn Abidin ؒ), *Sharh Lubāb al-Manasik, al-Ikhtiyar li ta'lil al-Mukhtār, Fatāwā 'Ālamgirī* and other authentic books [of Islamic jurisprudence (*Fiqh*)]: "Stand before Huzūr [the Messenger of Allah ﷺ] just as you stand in *Salāt*." (This is recorded in *Fatāwā 'Ālamgirī* and *al-Ikhtiyar*.) Shaykh 'Abdul Ghanī al-Maydanī ؒ in his *al-Lubāb* has said: "Stand reverentially with the hands folded by placing the right hand upon the left one."

17. Avoid kissing and touching the blessed trelliswork (*Jālī Mubārak*), as this is contrary to proper *Ādāb*.[138] The best practice is to stand four feet

---

[138] Imām Ahmad Razā ؒ disliked the practice of kissing and touching the graves. He said: "There are diverse opinions amongst the scholars regarding kissing graves. It is an act which lies between two things: something that allows the practice: love and something that disallows it: respect (*Adab*). Hence, the one who does it through overwhelming love is not criticized because this act is proven from the Companions (*Sahabah*). Though, it is better for the general public to be precautious. Our scholars have explicitly stated that one should stand at least four

away from the luminous Tomb (*Rauza al-Anwār*). Is it not sufficient for you that he ﷺ has been merciful enough to invite you into his sanctified court and permitted you to stand before him? Although his sight (*Nādhir*) was always upon you, but now you have been blessed with his mercy and special attention, and this [intimate] proximity has been conferred upon you.

18. Praise be to Allah! Your countenance like your heart is directly facing the *Jālī Mubārak* of the Messenger of Allah ﷺ, which is the resting place of the Beloved of Allah ﷺ. With the utmost *Ādāb* and personal humility, you should say with your eyes lowered in a soothing tone that is neither raised, nor inaudible: "Peace be upon you, O Prophet, and the mercy of Allah and His gracious favors! Peace be upon you, O Messenger of Allah! Peace be upon you, O Best of Creation! Peace be upon you, O Intercessor of the sinners! Peace be upon you, your noble Family, your illustrious Companions, and upon the entire Umma!"

---

feet away from the grave, so how would one kiss it!? (*Fatwa Ridhwiyah*, 9:528)." For further discussion of this topic, see Shaykh Monawwar Ateeq, "Practices at the graves of the scholars and righteous in the Indian Subcontinent and elsewhere."

Journey to the Holy House

The Razā family travelled by ship to return home, during their voyage they encountered a horrendous storm on the high seas that battered and tossed their vessel about for three days. The storm was so violent that the passengers gave up hope and put on their grave-clothes (*Kafan*). Imām Ahmad Razā ☙ was consoling his mother who was worried sick. He observed her with compassion, as she lamented the frightful prospect of a watery grave. He soothingly said, "Do not fret yourself mother. I swear by Allah that this ship will not sink." He said this with absolute certainty in the Hadīth Sharīf, for the Messenger of Allah ﷺ has assured those undertaking a journey protection if they recite the following supplication (*Du'ā*): **"Glory be to Him who has brought this (vehicle) under our control though we were unable to control it. Surely, we are to return to our Lord."**[139] A'lā Hazrat ☙ offered this supplication prior to boarding the ship; he had unshakable faith in the Hadīth Sharīf and continued to supplicate unto Allah and His Messenger ﷺ for help. As he continuously made this *Du'ā*, the storm slowly subsided, the ship made it to port safely, and everyone onboard was greatly

---

[139] Amina Baraka, *A Tribute to Shaikal-Islam As-Shaikh Imam Ahmad Raza* (Stockport: Raza Academy, 2005), 105.

relieved. But Imām Ahmad Razā ؓ never forgot the acute distress his mother felt during that voyage.[140]

A'lā Hazrat ؓ had tremendous respect for pilgrims, and made it a point to meet them whenever they returned from the Haramayn Sharīf. He would also inquire as to whether or not they visited the blessed Tomb (*Rauza al-Mubārak*) of our Master, Prophet Muhammad ﷺ. If the answer was yes, then he would kiss the Hājjī's feet. This act of self-effacement is indicative of one who loves the Prophet ﷺ more than anything else. Imām Ahmad Razā ؓ always honored the one who honored the Beloved ﷺ. Conversely, if the Hājjī's answer was no, then he would show his displeasure by ending the conversation.[141] Such love is only found among the pious servants (*Sālihīn*) of Allah Most Pure.

---

[140] Imām Mustafā Razā Khān, *al-Malfūz al-Sharīf*, 2:159.
[141] Mawlānā Muhammad Afthab Cassim, *Imam Ahmad Raza*, 93.

'Allāma Naqī's Union ﷺ

'Allāma Naqī 'Alī ﷺ preserved traditional Sunni scholarship, imparted theological instruction, and valiantly defended Islamic orthodoxy and mainstream Sufism. Like his father before him, 'Allāma Naqī ﷺ devoted every moment of his life to Allah and His Messenger ﷺ. With his last breath he uttered the Supreme Name (*Allah*) and slipped into the Divine Realm in the year 1297/1880. His most precious gift to the Community of Sayyidunā Muhammad ﷺ is without doubt Imām Ahmad Razā Khān al-Qādirī ﷺ, a Sunni's Sunni![142]

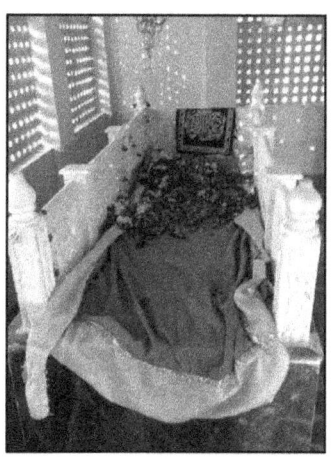

The tomb (*Mazār*) of 'Allāma Naqī in Bareilly, may Allah sanctify his secret and fill his grave with light, Āmīn.

---

[142] A Sunni's Sunni is a Muslim noted or admired for his traditionally Sunni interests and activities.

'Allāma Naqī willed his entire estate to A'lā Hazrat, who in turn would not touch a single rupee without asking his widowed mother's permission. He even sought her permission to purchase tomes of Sacred Knowledge; such was his love and reverence for her.[143] She devoted her entire life to serving his father and safeguarding his property, and the Imām in turn honored her for the remainder of her days as only a true spiritual son of the Prophet ﷺ could.

---

[143] Mawlānā Muhammad Afthab Cassim, *Imam Ahmad Raza*, 91.

The Birth of a Walī ﷺ

At this point something must be said about Imām Ahmad's younger son, Mustafā Razā Khān ؓ, who was born in the month of Dhul Hijjah 1310/1892. On the day of Mustafā Razā's birth, A'lā Hazrat ؓ was visiting the Barkātiyya Sayyids of Marehra. That day he dreamt of the child in his wife's womb and saw that it was a boy, whom he named Āl-e Rahmān (or, "The Vassal of the Most-Merciful"). A'lā Hazrat ؓ disclosed this dream to Hazrat Nūrī Miyān ؓ, who in turn named the boy Abu'l Barkāt Muhyi'd-dīn Jīlānī and promised to visit Bareilly Sharīf in the upcoming months. Later that year, he said to the boy's father: "This child will be of great assistance to the religion; and the pious servants of Allah will also benefit greatly through him, [because] this boy is a saint (*Walī*). Under his perceptive gaze thousands of stray Muslims will become firm in the religion for your son is a sea of blessings."[144]

---

[144] Mawlānā Muhammad Afthab Cassim, *The Chain of Light*, 2:141.

Reflections of Allah's Love

Then Hazrat Nūrī Miyān ﷺ placed his finger in the mouth of Mustafā Razā Khān ﷺ and made him a disciple (*Murīd*). He also entrusted this miraculous child with *Ijāzat* and *Khilāfat* in a single blow.[145] In the Sufi tradition this incident is reminiscent of the time when our Master Prophet Muhammad ﷺ placed his finger in the mouth of Asma' bint Abī Bakr's newborn son and named him 'Abdullāh ﷺ.[146] The Messenger of Allah ﷺ rubbed the infant's palate with his own blessed saliva, and a date that he had chewed himself. The Prophet ﷺ was the first Sufi, in all but name, and his inheritors (*Awliyā'*) actively follow his Sunnah by maintaining and reviving these forgotten aspects of Islamic worship.

Once Hazrat Dhoka Shāh—an "intoxicated" dervish,[147] whom Allah had drawn to Himself (*Majzūb*)—challenged Imām Ahmad Razā ﷺ and tested his love for the Master of

---

[145] Mawlānā Muhammad Afthab Cassim, *The Chain of Light*, 2:141.

[146] Sayyidunā 'Abdullāh ibn Zubayr ﷺ was the first child to be born in the illumined city of Medina. At the age of seven, he went to the Prophet ﷺ to pledge an oath of allegiance (*Bayat*). In the year seventy-three Hijrī, the Umayyad army besieged the ennobled city of Mecca. Although it was certain death, Abdullāh ibn Zubayr's beloved mother ﷺ wisely instructed her son to go out into battle against the Umayyad army and fight for truth. She asked him to exchange his armor for the robe of a martyr, since it is light and conceals that which must be kept hidden (*'Awra*). He dutifully obeyed his noble mother ﷺ, and was martyred at the age of seventy-two.

[147] This dervish was "intoxicated" with his Lord. It would be hard for most people to fathom his conduct or recognize his spiritual state.

The Birth of a Walī ؓ

the Messengers ﷺ. This well-known *Majzūb* said, "O Ahmad Razā! I am only able to see the authority of the Holy Prophet ﷺ on this earth. But not in the heavens." The Imām ؓ turned to face him, and replied, "The authority of the Messenger of Allah ﷺ is in the heavens and the earth." Again the *Majzūb* said he could not see it. So A'lā Hazrat said, "It is there, whether you can see it or not." Since the *Majzūb* was in highly spiritual state, he retorted, "Go! I have dropped him [referring to Mustafā Razā Khān ؓ, who was but a child playing atop the roof]." When the Imām reached his house, his mother counseled him and said, "You should know better than to quarrel with a *Majzūb*. Look! Mustafā Razā has fallen off the roof." A'lā Hazrat ؓ enquired about his son's health, when he was told that the boy was not injured he replied, "I am prepared to sacrifice a thousand sons for the pleasure of the Holy Prophet ﷺ, but I will not allow one word to be uttered against the dignity and honor of the most merciful Messenger ﷺ (*Rasūl al-Akram*).[148]

This one incident in A'lā Hazrat's sanctified life is rich with meaning: First and foremost, it reiterates the powerful Qur'ānic narrative and Ahādīth that teach us to succor and reverence the Messenger of Allah ﷺ. Next, it makes us recall stories of obedience and true love, which the lives of the Prophets and pious servants (*Sālihīn*) are

---

[148] Mawlānā Muhammad Afthab Cassim, *Imam Ahmad Raza*, 67.

replete with through their steadfastness to the command of Allah Most Pure. Wasn't Prophet Ibrāhīm ﷺ fully prepared to sacrifice his beloved son ﷺ? Wasn't his exalted son, the Prophet Ismā'īl ﷺ, a willing sacrifice for the sake of Allah? There is also a sound (*Sahīh*) Hadīth about a mother ﷺ who came to the Messenger of Allah ﷺ with nothing but her new born son, and implored him to take the boy as a human shield against the arrows of the non-believers. This valiant *sahābiyyah* ﷺ[149] was willing to sacrifice her own flesh and blood, the child of her womb to shield the Beloved of the Lord of all worlds ﷺ. All praise belongs to Allah alone! These are not children's stories or legends; these are actual accounts of the Prophets, Companions, and Sufi saints that teach us to heed the command of Allah, His Message, and His Messengers. Such narratives represent the zenith of faith. In all of these case studies the reader will also note that the venerable personalities in question were willing to make the ultimate sacrifice, yet Allah in His merciful Omniscience did not command them to carry out the act. The Sublime Lord confirmed their faith and honored them. Then He presented them with an agreeable alternative.

This anecdote from Imām Ahmad's life should teach us the importance of obedience to Allah and His Messenger ﷺ. He was completely effaced in the Real, and

---

[149] *Sahābiyyah*: A female companion of the Prophet ﷺ.

The Birth of a Walī

his "I" in this context is impersonal. It is the "I" of Allah that becomes the slave's ear with which he hears, his eye with which he sees, his hand with which he strikes, and his foot on which he walks. A holy utterance (*Hadīth Qudsī*) confirms the above: **"My slave does not draw closer to Me with anything more beloved to Me than that which I have made obligatory upon him. My slave continues to draw closer with supererogatory acts of devotion until I love him. When I love him, I am his hearing with which he hears, his sight with which he sees, his hand with which he grasps and his foot with which he walks. If he asks Me I will definitely give him, and if he seeks refuge with Me I will definitely give him refuge."**[150] In consequence, the *Majzūb's* defeat at the hands of A'lā Hazrat was actually a divine blessing for him. After some time, he returned to Imām Ahmad and said:

"O Ahmad Razā! You are victorious. Our case was presented before the Sultān of India (*Sultān al-Hind*), Hazrat Khawaja Gharīb Nawāz of Ajmer Sharīf (d. 627/1230), and he ruled in your favor. All praise belongs to Allah alone! Through the excellence of your grace I am now able to perceive

---

[150] Ibn Hajar al-'Asqalānī, *Selections from the Fath al-Bārī*, 17-18.

the beneficence (*Karam*) of the Holy Prophet ﷺ even in the heavens."[151]

Although somewhat aside from the general thesis of this book it must be said that had the command been to carry out the sacrifice there would still be no loss to the sacrificial lamb, only reward in the next world. This is evidenced from three miraculous accounts: The first is narrated on the authority of the Hanbalī Imām and Hadīth Master (*Hāfiz*) 'Abdul Rahmān ibn al-Jawzī ﷺ (d. 597/1201) in his book *'Uyun al-Hikāyāt* [The Fountain of Anecdotes], and pertains to three brothers who fought in the way of Allah against the Romans; they were captured, imprisoned and tortured. One day the Roman king came to them and said that he would set them free if they converted to Christianity. The brothers answered him by calling out, "O [Sayyidunā] Muhammad ﷺ!" This infuriated the king, who sentenced two of them to sudden death in boiling oil. The youngest brother was imprisoned indefinitely. But the Roman king was not victorious, for his daughter was drawn to this pious prisoner. She was mesmerized by his *Taqwā*, and remained close to him until she arranged for his escape and ran away with him. He faithfully conveyed the message of Islam to this noblewoman, who readily accepted it with all her heart

---

[151] Mawlānā Muhammad Afthab Cassim, *Imam Ahmad Raza*, 67.

and soul. Six months later they decided to marry. On the day of their celebration (*Nikāh*), the groom was wonderstruck, for amongst the guests he saw his two martyred brothers ushered in by a host of angels! Their physical presence was witnessed by everyone in attendance with absolute astonishment. His elder brothers were subsequently questioned about their death-defying feat to which they replied:

"When you (dear brother) saw us being thrown into the boiling oil, your eyes did not betray you for verily we entered that black cauldron of death. To you, however, it was the pot. But for us, it was admittance into the Gardens of Paradise (*Jannat al-Firdaus*)."[152]

The second and third account pertains to the martyrdom of Imām Husain ؇ and the Qur'ānic narrative of Prophet 'Īsā ibn Maryam ؇, respectively. When Yazīd's army ignobly beheaded the beloved grandson of the Messenger of Allah ؇ he was granted victory in Paradise. In this case, as the one before it, the apparent "victor" was the loser, and the one whose physical life was

---

[152] Imām Ahmad Razā Khān, "The Validity of Saying Yā Rasūlallāh ؇" in *Thesis of Imam Ahmad Raza* (Durban: Barkātur-Razā Publications, 2005), trans. Shaykh 'Abdul Hādī, 3:15-16.

Reflections of Allah's Love

lost won the next world! Those who are truly[153] martyred in the way of Allah are not dead. Rather: *they are alive!*[154] This is a startling secret known to the God-fearing.

This account is analogous in some respects to how the Jews were made to believe that they had crucified the Messiah, Jesus the son of Mary ﷺ. Allah, the Sublime and Exalted, has said: *And they did not slay him and they did not crucify him, but it seemed to them that they had done so.*[155] Prophet 'Īsā ibn Maryam ﷺ like Imām Husain ﷺ was victorious over his enemies. However, his story *is* unique, in that, his physically body was not molested and he has

---

[153] True *jihād* entails conforming to the rules of engagement as stipulated in the pure Sharī'ah. Our Prophet ﷺ forbid the killing of children, women, the elderly, monks (i.e., followers of other faiths, who are the custodians of temples, churches, and synagogues), and civilian non-combatants. The Master of Sharī'ah ﷺ did not condone vigilantism, terrorism, or anarchism under any pretext. Allah and His Messenger ﷺ have explicitly commanded us to: *Fight in the way of Allah those who fight you, but do not transgress the limits, for Allah loves not transgressors* (al-Qur'ān, 2:190). Abū Dāwūd relates from Anas ﷺ that the Prophet ﷺ said: **"Go in the Name of Allah and fight the enemy. But do not kill the elderly, children, or women. Do not be transgressors, for Allah loves those who keep the highest standards of discipline and do not harm people (*Muhsinīn*)."** What some Muslims are doing today in the name of Islam under the banner of *"jihād"* is absolutely criminal. Islam does not condone violence in the name of religion. The lesser *jihād* is permissible in a situation of legitimate self-defense, such as when an intruder enters one's home to steal or otherwise harm its occupants, or in a lawful situation of combat between two armies.
[154] Al-Qur'ān, 2:154.
[155] Al-Qur'ān, 4:156-157.

The Birth of a Walī ﷺ

not yet breathed his last, rather Allah raised him up to Himself. That is why Jesus the son of Mary ﷺ will return in the Last Days to reaffirm the true message of Islam, and bear witness that Sayyidunā Muhammad ﷺ is the Seal of the Prophets (*Khātam an-Nabiyyīn*). He will rule according to the Divine Law established by the Messenger of Allah ﷺ; and the Muslims will pray the funeral prayer over him when he finally takes his last breath in this transient world.

Let us now return to the personal narrative of this young *Walī* of Allah, who grew to become an eminent Muftī of the Indian Subcontinent and scholar par excellence like his father ﷺ. Shaykh Mustafā Razā Khān al-Qādirī ﷺ is popularly known as *al-Muftī al-A'zam Hind* (or, "The Supreme Muftī of India").[156] His primary education was obtained at Dār al-'Ulūm Manzar al-Islām (Bareilly), where he studied under some of the most distinguished scholars of his time, including his elder brother, Hujjat al-Islām Shaykh Hāmid Razā Khān al-Qādirī ﷺ, *Ustādh al-Asātidha* (or, "The Teacher of the Teachers") 'Allāma Shāh

---

[156] Shaykh Mustafā ﷺ is considered by many highly distinguished *Mashā'ikh* and *'Ulamā* to be a Renewer (*Mujaddid*) of the 15th Islamic century.

Reflections of Allah's Love

Raham Ilāhī Maglorī ☙, *Shaykh al-'Ulamā* (or, "The Shaykh of the Scholars") Sayyid Bashīr Ahmad 'Aligarhī ☙, and *Shāms al-'Ulamā* (or, "The Sun of the Scholars") Zahūr al-Hussain Rampurī ☙.

Shaykh Mustafā mastered thirty-six Islamic sciences by his eighteenth birthday. He was in the constant habit of praying and punctually performed the ritual prayers in congregation, even whilst traveling. His tongue was always moist with the remembrance of Allah (*Dhikr*), especially when writing talismans for the masses that flocked to him. He became proficient in several subtle forms of *Dhikr* that are known to the elect as well. He authored more than thirty books, including several outstanding works on Islamic doctrine (*'Aqīdah*) and jurisprudence (*Fiqh*). A prime example of this genius is seen in his answer to a question regarding Islamic spirituality (*Tasawwuf*), a man once asked him: "O Huzūr! Is it permissible to remember one's Shaykh during the ritual prayer?" He replied: "If you need to remember anyone in prayer, then you should remember the Beloved of Allah ☙. Yet if the thought of one's spiritual guide comes to mind, in the same way the gaze of a person wanders from here to there, then there is no hindrance."[157]

---

[157] Mawlānā Muhammad Afthab Cassim, *Huzoor Mufti-e-Azam Hind ☙: A Steadfast & Miraculous Personaity* (Durban: Imam Mustafa Research Centre, 2007), 44.

The Birth of a Walī ﷺ

Our body, mind, and soul should be fixed upon Allah and His Messenger ﷺ, but it is not forbidden for one to be absorbed momentarily in the thought of the physical guide, who is in fact taking us to "The Guide" (*Al-Hādī*).

Imām Ahmad ﷺ in his *al-Kaukabah ash-Shihābiyyah* [The Scorching Star][158] exclaimed: "O Muslims! Does not the recital of *at-Tahiyāt*[159] provide a direct injunction to contemplate the Best of Creation ﷺ in the midst of *Salāt*? Verily it does, and undoubtedly the thought of him will overwhelm our hearts with magnificence and grandeur, as meditation upon him is sealed with his unique specialty, and saluting such a [peerless] personality is in reality remembering and honoring him, so the explicit injunction [to perform *at-Tahiyāt*] is not only a salutation of greeting, but also honoring and magnifying his blessed being in the state of prayer (*Salāt*). Allah has said: *But the hypocrites know not* [63:8]. Imām Abū Hāmid al-Ghazzālī ﷺ

---

[158] This is a paraphrased summation that remains faithful to the general meaning of the original work, but not to the exact wording of the text. For a precise translation of the Urdu into contemporary English prose, please read Hājī Tehsīn Razā Hamdanī's *The Scorching Star*, available at www.thesunniway.com. Hājī Sāhib included useful endnotes and extensive references that are a great resource to English-speaking Muslims. The author wishes to thank Hājī Sāhib for giving her permission to make slight modifications to his work.

[159] The Majestic Lord necessitated the recital of *at-Tahiyāt* at the end of every two cycles of prayer, wherein there is a compulsion to say: "Greetings to Allah, and peace be upon you, O Prophet, and likewise the mercy and blessings of Allah."

Reflections of Allah's Love

in his *Ihyā' 'Ulūm ad-Dīn* says: 'In *at-Tahiyāt* acknowledge the presence of the Prophet ﷺ and contemplate his blessed countenance; thereafter recite: *As-salāmun 'alayka*[160] *ayyunha'n-Nabīyyu wa rahmatullāhī wa-barakātuhu.*"[161] On the previous page of *al-Kaukabah ash-Shihābiyyah*, A'lā Hazrat poetically proclaimed: "All praise is due to Allah alone, the glory of Sayyidunā Muhammad ﷺ is higher and more immense than the Throne of Allah, and no one can extinguish it. Assuredly, the baying of the hounds does not diminish the splendor of the moonlight.

See how the moonlight reveals the true nature of things, for the dogs are howling at the brilliance of the moon."[162]

---

[160] Shaykh Muhammad al-Yaqūbī in his talk on *The Slave & The Master* explains how the Messenger of Allah ﷺ is central to our life and worship (*'Ibādah*). In track four of this audio lecture, he too says: "But also we understand that in the prayer itself, before the end of the prayer, we say *As-salāmun 'alayka ayyunha'n-Nabīyyu wa rahmatullāhī wa-barakātuhu*. A prayer devoted to Allah ﷻ, but leaves some remove to address Rasūlu'llāh ﷺ, to turn the heart to him, to turn the mind to him, to visualize him in front of you, so that you address him with careful *khtāb 'alayka*, not *'alayhi*, peace be upon you, not peace be upon him, *As-salāmun 'alayka ayyunha'n-Nabīyyu wa rahmatullāhī wa-barakātuhu*. This is in the prayer."

[161] Imām Ahmad Razā Khān, *al-Kaukabah ash-Shihābiyyah* [The Scorching Star], trans. Hājī Tehsīn Razā Hamdanī, accessed on December 29, 2011, http://thesunniway.com/index.php/files/file/645-the-scorching-star-on-infidelities-of-the-father-of-wahaabism/, 35.

[162] Ibid., 34.

The Birth of a Walī ؑ

Shaykh Mustafā ؑ was his father's son; and the Bountiful Lord blessed him with a long life for the benefit of the Prophet's ﷺ Community. If Allah so wills, we intend to come back to the personal narrative of Muftī al-A'zam Hind ؑ as the biography of Imām Ahmad Razā Khān al-Qādirī ؑ develops.

A Towering Figure

Imām Ahmad's ﷺ stature was elevated to even greater heights as he sat at the feet of prominent scholars and jurists form his native India and the Haramayn. This remarkable young man specialized in over fifty branches of knowledge, including Qur'ānic exegesis (*Tafsīr*), Hadīth, applied jurisprudence (*Fiqh*), the principles of jurisprudence (*Usul al-Fiqh*), doctrine (*'Aqīdah*), rational theology (*Kalam*), Islamic mysticism (*Tasawwuf*), syntax (*Nahw*), etymology (*Sarf*), history, logic, philosophy, astronomy, astrology, and mathematics.[163] His sagacious knowledge was complemented by an impeccable character and comportment. Being in the presence of A'lā Hazrat ﷺ was a constant reminder of our Prophet's ﷺ words: **"Surely, Allah will send for this Umma at the advent of every one hundred years a person (or persons) who will**

---

[163] Maryam Qadri, *The Voice of Truth: A'la Hazrat Mujaddid Imam Ahmed Raza* (Martinsville: Al-Mukhtar Books, 2010), 3-4.

A Towering Figure

renew its religion for it."[164] The 'Ulamā of his day could not help but notice that he was a towering figure in the annuals of religious renewal. He revitalized the Community of Sayyidunā Muhammad ﷺ through his nobility, scrupulousness, and memorable presence.

It was shortly after the publication of *Fatāwā al-Haramayn* [The Edicts of the Sacred Sanctuaries][165] in 1900 that the scholars of the Subcontinent declared Imām Ahmad ؓ to be a Renewer (*Mujaddid*) of the 14th Islamic century.[166] The announcement occurred at Madrasa Hanafiyyah in the city of Patna. One of the speakers present referred to A'lā Hazrat as the *"Mujaddid* of the present century." Those in attendance gave their unconditional support, and later thousands of others conferred this accolade upon him as well, to such a degree that there seemed to be a consensus among the Sunni 'Ulamā of British India on the question.[167]

He was again declared a *Mujaddid* by the 'Ulamā in Mecca the Ennobled and Medina the Illumined in

---

[164] Muftī Jalāl ad-Dīn Ahmad al-Qādirī al-Amjadī, *In Light of the Sacred Traditions of the Beloved* ﷺ, 84.
[165] The full title of Imām Ahmad's edict is *Fatāwā al-Haramayn bi Rajf Nadwat al-Mayn* [Edicts of the Sacred Sanctuaries shaking the lying council].
[166] This edict was endorsed by sixteen leading scholars from Mecca the Ennobled.
[167] Sanyal, *Ahmad Riza Khan Barelwi*, 65.

Reflections of Allah's Love

1323/1905 after the publication of two glorious masterpieces, namely, *Husām al-Haramayn* [The Sword of the Sacred Sanctuaries]—a *Fatwā* that was certified by twenty scholars from Mecca and thirteen from Medina; and represented the view of three juristic schools of Sunni law (namely the Hanafī, Shāfi'ī, and Mālikī)—and *ad-Dawlah al-Makkiyyah bi'l Māddati'l Ghaybiyyah* [The Meccan Realm on the Matter of the Unseen], a definitive treatise on the Prophet's 🌺 knowledge of the unseen which received seventy-seven endorsements from the scholars of Hijaz, Yemen, Syria, and Egypt.

Accurately commenting on the marks of respect and deference shown to A'lā Hazrat 🌺 and his scholarly opinion by the Haramayn 'Ulamā, South Asian historian Dr. Usha Sanyal writes, "We might even say that relations between center and periphery, Mecca and India, had been reversed during Ahmad Riza's three-month stay."[168] One scholar said of him, "Although he was a Hindi [an Indian], his light was shining in Mecca."[169] Top-ranking Meccan scholars declared him to be the *Mujaddid* of the 20th century,[170] whilst their venerable counterparts in Medina the Illumined referred to him as the *Mujaddid* of the

---

[168] Sanyal, *Ahmad Riza Khan Barelwi*, 73.
[169] Ibid.
[170] *Mujaddid al-Mi'ah al-Hadirah*

A Towering Figure

Community,[171] and the *Mujaddid* of the century[172] as well. Imām Ahmad's biographer and deputy (*Khalīfah*) Muftī Muhammad Zafar ad-Dīn Bihārī ؓ was not exaggerating when he said that his beloved teacher and Murshid al-Kāmil ؓ fulfilled all the requirements of a *Mujaddid*, and that he was the "most famous among the celebrated of his age."[173] Even today prominent Sunni scholars like Shaykh Sayyid Abu'l Hudā Muhammad al-Yaqūbī of Syria (b. 1382/1963) have noted that Imām Ahmad was a *Mujaddid*, and the most famous of all scholars of modern times in the Indian Subcontinent, and a great bounty from Allah for the people of South Asia.[174]

One of the many hallmarks of a *Mujaddid* is that he be a profound Sufi that typifies the Prophetic Sunnah. Imām Ahmad ؓ was such a Sufi who never underestimated the value of kindness and spiritual courtesy (*Ādāb*). He would even show compassion and tolerance to those with mistaken notions, as the following anecdotes clearly admit. Once a *hāfiz* of the Qur'ān introduced a young man

---

[171] *Mujaddid hadhihil Umma*
[172] *Mujaddid al-Qarn*
[173] Sanyal, *Ahmad Riza Khan Barelwi*, 65.
[174] These remarks were made during a live *Takbeer TV* interview that aired on the 21st of Rajab 1431, which corresponds to July 3, 2010. A transcript of this talk is available at http://www.sunniport.com/books/transcript%20shaykh%20yaqubi%20on%20alahazrat.pdf (last accessed on April 7, 2012), 2-3. One may watch the segment on Imām Ahmad Razā by visiting http://www.youtube.com/watch?v=b92u3Rh7oUc.

Reflections of Allah's Love

to Imām Ahmad ﷺ, for his friend had some erroneous views that required clarification. After a brief dialogue with the Imām, the gentleman got up, said his goodbyes, and left. Later the *hāfiz* met with A'lā Hazrat and proclaimed: "Esteemed Shaykh! When my friend left you, he said that his heart was satisfied by your good counsel. He intends to become your disciple very soon, if Allah so wills."[175]

Imām Ahmad was a gentle soul, who genuinely believed in the power of kindness. This was one of his core teachings, which he imparted to his students. Had he reproached this gentleman, it would have made him firm in his faults. In the words of the Imām, "Always remember this golden rule: When someone is in a state of spiritual and intellectual confusion be [exceedingly] patient with him and give him more attention. Shower him in love and kindness, because this will [positively] affect him. But the opposite is true in the case of hardcore Wahhābīs, who were met first with kindness and yet their arrogance was such that they refused to accept the truth.[176] In consequence, the scholar-saints put pen to paper and waged (intellectual) *jihād* against their deviation and

---

[175] Imām Mustafā Razā Khān, *al-Malfūz al-Sharīf*, 1:47.
[176] A'lā Hazrat ﷺ made it a point to warn the reader about Wahhābīs, and the utter futility of being tactful with them. He admonished Sunni Muslims not to associate with Wahhābīs and to avoid any form of debate or dialogue with them.

A Towering Figure

heresy."[177] There is a saying attributed to our Prophet ﷺ that: **"The ink of the scholar is dearer than the blood of the martyr; on the Day of Resurrection, the former shall be weighed against the latter and outweigh it."**[178]

There is an analogous example to this anecdote in the life of Prophet Muhammad ﷺ. Once a Companion came to him and said: "O Messenger of Allah! Make adultery (*Zinā*) permissible for me." Some of the Companions (*Ashāb*) were outraged by his request and were prepared to unsheathe their swords. But the Messenger of Allah ﷺ stopped them, and asked the first Companion to sit down before him, knee-to-knee. The one who was sent *as a Mercy for all creatures* ﷺ[179] inquired: **"Would you like someone to commit adultery with your mother?"** And the Companion answered: "No." Then the Prophet ﷺ asked if he would like someone to commit adultery with his daughter, sister, or aunt. And the Companion's reply was the same. At last, the noble Prophet ﷺ said: **"The woman with whom you intend to commit adultery will be a mother, or a daughter, or a sister, or an aunt (of your brother). Do not do to others that which you would not**

---

[177] Imām Mustafā Razā Khān, *al-Malfūz al-Sharīf*, 1:47-48.
[178] Although the meaning holds true, one of the most eminent Hadīth scholars, al-Khatīb, in his *Tārikh* said it is forged.
[179] The Exalted has described the Prophet ﷺ as *most merciful and kind to the Believers* (9:128), and *as a Mercy for all creatures* (21:107).

want others to do to you."[180] After speaking these inspired words, the Messenger of Allah ﷺ struck his Companion on the chest and offered the following supplication: **"O Allah! Remove the desire to commit adultery from his heart."** When this Companion first went to the Prophet ﷺ there was nothing more beloved to him than adultery, but after receiving his compassionate touch adultery became vile to him.[181]

Allah's Messenger ﷺ addressed this Companion again, saying: **"The example between you and me is like a camel that breaks loose and runs away. The owner of the camel says, 'Leave it! I know what it needs.' He then offers the camel an olive branch, which it considers from a safe distance. The owner approaches the disturbed camel slowly, and convinces it to rest. Thereafter, the owner mounts his camel and guides it home."**[182] Our Prophet ﷺ cautioned the other Companions against being quick to anger and the sword. He admonished his Community to be tolerant, merciful, compassionate, and kind—especially to those whose understanding differs from our own.

Imām Ahmad was a master of the Science of Premonition (*'Ilm al-Jafr*), one day Pīrzada Hazrat Sayyid

---

[180] Imām Mustafā Razā Khān, *al-Malfūz al-Sharīf*, 1:48-49.
[181] Ibid., 1:49.
[182] Ibid.

A Towering Figure

Mehdī Hasan ﷺ sent him a question from Marehra Sharīf that concerned the health of a wealthy woman from a Sh'īa household. A'lā Hazrat received the following answer to this highborn woman's predicament: "Follow the correct path of the People of the Sunnah [*Ahl al-Sunnah*], or else there is no cure." As a rule, the answer must be given as clearly as it was received from the subtle realm. This science does not permit its researchers to withhold information from those who ask, nor does it permit alterations to the premonition one receives. The Imām recorded this prescription, and dispatched it to Marehra Sharīf forthwith.[183]

Unfortunately, the family was displeased with his answer and sent another question by way of Sayyid Mehdī, which queried: "When and where will she die in the city of Nainital or her hometown?" Ninital is a popular hill station in the Indian state of Uttarakhand; and she had been residing there for medical reasons. Their question reached Imām Ahmad on the 8th of Shawwāl, 1328/1910. Another answer came from the subtle realm, which predicted that her death would occur in her hometown close to her residence in the month of Muharram. As before the family disregarded the Imām's insight, but his prediction was confirmed down to the minutest detail

---

[183] Imām Mustafā Razā Khān, *al-Malfūz al-Sharīf*, 2:199-200.

when she passed away in a garden near her own home in Muharram.¹⁸⁴

One of the most salient features of this story is how a staunch Sunni like A'lā Hazrat ؓ was willing to help those in need, even though they had some mistaken notions, for Allah says: *Call to the way of your Lord with wisdom and fair exhortation, and argue with them in ways that are best and most gracious.*¹⁸⁵ All saints being the Friends of Allah follow the dictum of the Spiritual Sovereign of India (*Sultān al-Hind*), Khwāja Mu'īn ad-Dīn Chishtī ؓ (d. 627/1230), who avowed that a true Friend of Allah must shine upon all like the sun; he must be magnanimous like a river and possess the humility of the earth.¹⁸⁶ Al-Bayhaqī ؓ in his *Shu'ab al-Īmān* relates that our Prophet ﷺ said: **"All creatures are Allah's dependents, and the most beloved of creation to Allah is the one who is benevolent to His dependents."**¹⁸⁷ It has also been narrated on the authority of Mullā 'Alī al-Qārī ؓ in his *Mirqāt al-Mafātīh* that our Master Prophet Muhammad ﷺ said: **"The best of you is the one who is the most helpful to others."**¹⁸⁸

---

¹⁸⁴ Imām Mustafā Razā Khān, *al-Malfūz al-Sharīf*, 2:200.

¹⁸⁵ Al-Qur'ān, 16:125.

¹⁸⁶ This saying is the essence of Khwāja Sāhib's ؓ teaching which has been recorded in several books of *Tasawwuf*. For further information, visit http://www.gharibnawaz.com/g_teachings.htm.

¹⁸⁷ Related by al-Bayhaqī in his *Shu'ab al-Īmān*.

¹⁸⁸ Narrated by Mullā 'Alī al-Qārī in his *Mirqāt al-Mafātīh sharh Mishkāt al-Masābīh*.

A Towering Figure

Imām Ahmad kept Sufism well-within the framework of Islamic law. He was a scholar-saint comparable to leading exemplars of prophetic love and religious revival, including Shaykh Yūsuf ibn Ismā'īl an-Nabahānī ؓ (d. 1350/1931) and Imām Abū Hāmid al-Ghazzālī ؓ (d. 505/1111). He vehemently opposed the call for unity among Sunnis and deviant sects that oppose the Sunnah. Much of his ministry was devoted exclusively to protecting the creed of the *Ahl al-Sunnah*, and safeguarding Muslims from those who ally themselves with misguidance, for example, when asked if Muslims should fraternize with atheists and progressive reformers, A'lā Hazrat replied by quoting a Hadīth Sharīf that said: **"Run away from them and keep them away from you, so that they do not mislead you."**[189] Sayyidunā ash-Shaykh Muhyi'd-dīn 'Abdul Qādir al-Jīlānī ؓ quotes a similar report from 'Abdul Rahmān ibn 'Umar ؓ in an appendix on "sects that have gone astray" in his *Sufficient Provision for Seekers of the Path of Truth*, in which Allah's Messenger ؐ said: **"The counsel I bequeath to you is dutiful devotion [*taqwā*] to Allah, and paying heed and obedience [to your leader], even if he happens to be an**

---

[189] Imām Mustafā Razā Khān, *al-Malfūz al-Sharīf*, 2:309.

Abyssinian slave, for anyone who lives on after me will experience much disharmony. You must therefore strive to follow my exemplary practice [*sunnatī*], and the exemplary practice of the rightly guided Caliphs [*sunnat al-khulafā' ar-rāshidīn*] after I am gone. You must hold on to it with a very tight grip, and doggedly sink your teeth into it. You must beware of novel fashions [*muhdathāt al-umūr*], for every novelty is a heretical innovation [*bid'a*], and every heretical innovation is a deviation from the right path."[190]

This question concerning atheists and sects beyond the pale of Sunni beliefs was asked to the *Mujaddid* in the city of Jabalpur on a Friday (the 27th of Rajab, 1337/1919) at the time of the afternoon prayer (*Salāt al-'Asr*). Imām Ahmad had treated those in attendance to an eloquent exhortation on why preserving the Sunni identity is vital, which affected the congregation so powerfully that echoes of repentance (*Tawba*) were heard from all sides. One man was so moved by it that he actually fell at the Imām's feet and begged for forgiveness. A'lā Hazrat responded by saying, "Beloved brothers! This is a time when Allah's Mercy descends upon His servants. Let us all repent to the Most Merciful and Compassionate Lord. Repent secretly for those sins committed in secret, and repent publicly for

---

[190] Shaykh 'Abdul Qādir al-Jīlānī, *Sufficient Provision for Seekers of the Path of Truth*, 1:396.

A Towering Figure

those sins committed in public. The pure Sharī'ah urges us to repent immediately when we commit a sin, secretly for our hidden transgressions and publicly for our open ones." Tears streamed from the eyes of those in attendance and some, who were lost in a state of spiritual ecstasy (*Wajd*), began to scream. Imām Ahmad wept profusely with them. There is little doubt that their tears washed away most of their past sins. People threw themselves at the Imām's feet, as this humble servant of the Chosen One ﷺ prayed for their forgiveness. All praise belongs to Allah alone, the Ever-Forgiving One![191]

In the following year (1901), the *Mujaddid* of the 14th Islamic century completed *Kanz al-Īmān* [A Treasury of Faith]. This book is an authoritative translation of the Qur'ān into the Urdu language that can also be utilized as an exegesis (*Tafsīr*). *Kanz* means "to treasure, treasuring, hoarding; a treasure, store." It seems as though the author was telling us to treasure our faith in the Word of Allah, and hold onto it. Abū Dharr ؓ relates that the Prophet ﷺ said: **"Recite the Qur'ān for it will be light for you on the earth and a treasure for you in the heaven."**[192] Perhaps this Hadīth Sharīf came to mind when he was selecting the

---

[191] Imām Mustafā Razā Khān, *al-Malfūz al-Sharīf*, 2:309-311.
[192] Mullā 'Alī al-Qārī, *Forty Hadīth on the Excellence of the All-Clarifying Illuminating Qur'ān* (Kitaba: Glasgow, 2008), trans. Abdul Aziz Ahmed, 22.

title of his Urdu translation, and Allah knows best. Few would be better qualified for the task of interpreting the Holy Qu'rān.

A'lā Hazrat ﷺ was well-versed in classical Arabic, etymology and syntax (*Sarf-o-Nahw*). He also followed a seven day course for the complete recitation (*Khatm*) of the Book of Allah, which means he recited the entire Qur'ān at least fifty-two times a year. In *A Collection of Prayers & Invocations*, Imām Ahmad reminds us that there is no better litany (*Wazīfah*) than that of the continuous recitation of the Holy Qur'ān.[193] It was imperative to him that his disciples recite at least one *Sūrah* a day,[194] whilst aspiring to undertake this weekly reading through the blessings of the Friends of Allah.[195]

---

[193] Imām Ahmad Razā Khān, *A Collection of Prayers & Invocations* [al-Wazīfat al-Karīmah] (Martinsville: Al-Mukhtār Books, 2012), trans. Muhammad Kalīm al-Qādirī, 108-109.
[194] Ibid., 56.
[195] Ibid., 108-109.

Regard for Women

Imām Ahmad's regard for women is best illustrated by three events in his life: One transpired before his second Hajj, and the other two occurred in the midst of his Pilgrimage. These anecdotes enable us to regale the reader with the story of A'lā Hazrat's monumental second Hajj as well. The first incident concerns his beloved mother ⚘. It bears mentioning that mothers enjoy an elevated status in Islam.[196] This right is given to all parents (Muslim and non-Muslim), for our Lord has decreed: *Do not worship anyone but Him, and be good to your parents. If one or both of them attain old-age in your presence, do not say fie to them, nor reprove them, but address them with words of honor. And look after them with kindness and love, and say: 'O Lord, have mercy on them as they nourished me when I was small.'*[197] Our Prophet ﷺ has made it abundantly clear that: **"Paradise**

---

[196] For further discussion of this topic, see Muftī Muhammad Nizāmuddīn Razvī Misbahī, *The Elevated Status of Parents* (Bolton: Maktab-e-Qadriah, n.d.), trans. Sadia Mehmood.
[197] Al-Qur'ān, 17:23-24.

lies at the mother's feet."[198] And that the parent with the greatest claim over us with regard to service and kind treatment is: "**Your mother, and again your mother, and once again your mother. After her is the claim of your father.**"[199]

Several members of the Razā household, including the Imām's younger brother, Mawlānā Muhammad Razā (d. 1357/1939), and his son, Shaykh Hāmid ﷺ, were departing for the Pilgrimage in 1323/1905, so A'lā Hazrat ﷺ accompanied them till Lucknow. After dropping them off at the railway station he returned home to Bareilly totally dejected, as the thought of Hajj and visiting the blessed Tomb of our Master, the Messenger of Allah ﷺ, was foremost in his mind. But as fate would have it, his beloved mother ﷺ greeted him at the door, and the first words to escape her lips were, "You have already performed your obligatory (*Fard*) Hajj by the grace of Allah Most Pure. Now do not intend to go again during my lifetime."[200]

But the Imām's desire was so intense that he was unable to concentrate, and as the week wore on it only seemed to worsen. On the one hand, he was yearning to

---

[198] Muftī Jalāl ad-Dīn Ahmad al-Qādirī al-Amjadī, *In Light of the Sacred Traditions of the Beloved* ﷺ, 362.
[199] Muftī Muhammad Nizāmuddīn Razvī Misbahī Sāhib Qibla, *The Elevated Status of Parents*, 61.
[200] Imām Mustafā Razā Khān, *al-Malfūz al-Sharīf*, 2:160.

Regard for Women

visit the Holy House and the Meadow (*Rawda*) of the Prophet ﷺ. On the other hand, he required his mother's consent to perform a supererogatory (*Nāfil*) Hajj, and she had already given her opinion on the matter. A'lā Hazrat ؓ did not know what to do; he was torn between his mother's request and his heart's desire.[201]

When he could not bear this torture any longer he decided to purchase a ticket for Mumbai and beseech his noble mother for her blessings and permission. He was fully cognizant of the fact that without her consent it would be unlawful (*Harām*) for him to take a single step toward the ennobled city of Mecca. Thus after saying the afternoon prayer ('*Asr*), A'lā Hazrat ؓ made persistent supplications to undertake the Pilgrimage. Resigning himself to the will of Allah, the Sublime and Exalted, Imām Ahmad ؓ wistfully approached his mother's bedside and placed his head upon her feet. She immediately sat up and said, "What is it?" He replied with utmost humility, "Please grant me permission to perform the Pilgrimage [without undue delay]." "Allah [be your] protector (*Khudā hāfiz*)," was her reply. Upon hearing these two precious words A'lā Hazrat ؓ hastened to the train station. The mercy of Allah was upon His sincere supplicant. Before leaving home, Imām Ahmad ؓ performed a complete ablution (*Kāmil Wudū*) with

---

[201] Imām Mustafā Razā Khān, *al-Malfūz al-Sharīf*, 2:160-161.

tremendous joy, deep devotion, and immense gratitude (*Shukr*). His mother kept his ablution water with her until his return; and she would often look upon it and say, "This was his *Wudū* water."²⁰²

Imām Ahmad ؓ sent a telegram from Bareilly station to Mumbai letting his family know that he was on his way, but the recipients' presumed it was from A'lā Hazrat's brother, Shaykh Hasan Razā Khān al-Qādirī ؓ (d. 1326/1908).²⁰³ Since the latter had made provisions to go for Hajj last year, whilst the spontaneity of the former took everyone by surprise. Imām Ahmad's train was supposed to link up with one headed to Mumbai from Agra, but it was delayed by several days. He was very anxious to reach Mumbai as it was already Thursday and all the *Hujjāj* in this ancient seaport city were getting ready to be temporarily quarantined for their departure. It seemed as though the odds were stacked against him, as the ship and its passengers must have been making preparations to set sail.²⁰⁴

---

²⁰² Imām Mustafā Razā Khān, *al-Malfūz al-Sharīf*, 2:161.
²⁰³ Shaykh Hasan ؓ is also known as "The Preceptor of the Time" (*Ustād al-Zamān*).
²⁰⁴ Imām Mustafā Razā Khān, *al-Malfūz al-Sharīf*, 2:161-162.

Regard for Women

This delay, however, proved to be providential and enabled a throng of devoted followers to meet A'lā Hazrat ﷺ at the Mumbai train station. After meeting his well-wishers, Hājī Qāsim arranged for a car to take the celebrated Muftī directly to the docks. It was eight o'clock on a Friday morning when Imām Ahmad ﷺ finally reached the port of Mumbai. The passengers had not yet boarded the ship, thus he was able to complete the bureaucratic red tape and join his family and friends in their quarantine quarters. A'lā Hazrat ﷺ immediately extolled the Lord of the worlds and gave Him thanks (*Shukr*)![205]

Imām Ahmad ﷺ asked the group why their period of confinement was prolonged. They replied, "It was an unprecedented turn of events. The doctor was punctual in examining the quarantined passengers, and had checked about half of them when suddenly he felt very ill and behaved in an unusual manner. He left us [abruptly] saying the remaining passengers will be examined tomorrow." Although A'lā Hazrat ﷺ had made it for the mandatory health inspection, he was faced with another formidable obstacle, in that, he did not have a ticket to travel on this particular ship, and all the seats were sold out. After making an inquiry, their Hajj group was told that there was only one seat left on the next ship, and it

---

[205] Imām Mustafā Razā Khān, *al-Malfūz al-Sharīf*, 2:162.

was a third class ticket. The Razā family rarely travelled by third class, but the unseen hand of divine providence was at work. Imām Ahmad ﷺ solemnly purchased the ticket as it meant he would be undertaking the voyage alone without his kith and kin.[206]

In characteristic fashion he turned to the One, the Unique, the Munificent, the Bestower, and read the supplications given to us by His beloved Messenger ﷺ in the Hadīth Sharīf, begging the Lord Almighty for the companionship of his friends and relations on this most sacred journey. The other members of his group began looking for someone in a similar situation, who would be willing to trade places with the Imām. The Bountiful Lord made it easy for His slave and granted him assistance. Amongst the pilgrims there was an old man from the district of Bareilly, who readily exchanged his seat with the *Mujaddid*.

With much gratitude A'lā Hazrat ﷺ considered this incident to be a miracle (*Karāmāt*) from Allah through the *tawassul* of His Chosen One ﷺ with whom He is well pleased. For the elderly man could only afford a third class ticket, which meant that if the Imām was able to procure a first or second class ticket, then the two gentlemen from Bareilly would be unable to exchange seats! Their transaction went smoothly and neither

---

[206] Imām Mustafā Razā Khān, *al-Malfūz al-Sharīf*, 2:162.

Regard for Women

passenger was inconvenienced by the grace of Allah and His Messenger ﷺ. Imām Ahmad glorified his Creator with the words, "All praise and thanks belongs to Allah alone!" Once the health inspection was complete, everyone boarded the ship that set sail for Jeddah.[207]

It was time for the afternoon prayer (*'Asr*) when the pilgrims reached Aden, a famous seaport city in Yemen. One of the passengers, a disgruntled Arab man, kept on complaining that they were facing the wrong diction in *Salāt*. However prior to performing the ritual prayer, Imām Ahmad ؓ had personally ascertained the direction of the *Qibla*. After saying the prayer and completing all of his litanies and invocations (*Wazā'if*), he asked this gentleman about the direction of the *Qibla* and if its direction had changed in the last five minutes. The Arab man was unable to answer A'lā Hazrat's questions, so the Imām politely showed him how to ascertain the direction of the *Qibla* at sea. This simple clarification resulted in an accord between the two.[208]

The pilgrims had to disembark at Jeddah for a quarantine inspection before being permitted to enter the seaport city. Unfortately, some mean-spirited policemen took it upon themselves to be a positive nuisance. But Allah Alimghty tests us through ease and hardship *and*

---

[207] Imām Mustafā Razā Khān, *al-Malfūz al-Sharīf*, 2:162-163.
[208] Ibid., 2:163.

*with hardship there is ease.*²⁰⁹ Accordingly, the pilgrims resigned themselves to their fate with patient endurance and absolute trust in Allah knowing that He would surely expiate their sins and elevate their ranks through this ordeal. The pilgrims were cooped up for more than nine days, and were attended to by doctors from Turkey. Imām Ahmad ؓ asked Allah Most Pure to bless their Turkish physicians, who made the pilgrims feel at home and took excellent care of them.²¹⁰

One of the passengers informed A'lā Hazrat ؓ that a mausoleum of a great Sufi saint was in close proximity to their camp. Upon hearing this good news Imām Ahmad was anxious to visit the Walī's sanctified tomb, but no one could leave their encampment. He approached a Turkish doctor who surprisingly granted his entire entourage (approximately ten to twelve pilgrims) permission to go outside of the quarantine line. They visited the blessed mausoleum and derived untold spiritual grace (*Fayd*) from the noble soul (*Rūh*) resting in Aden.²¹¹

Throughout their period of solitary confinement, Imām Ahmad ؓ delivered lectures on the Fiqh of Hajj with special emphasis on increasing the pilgrims love and

---

²⁰⁹ Al-Qur'ān, 94:5-6.
²¹⁰ Imām Mustafā Razā Khān, *al-Malfūz al-Sharīf*, 2:163.
²¹¹ Ibid.

reverence for the Messenger of Allah ﷺ. One of the attendees would listen with rapt attention to the laws of Hajj, but his face would sour whenever A'lā Hazrat ؓ praised Allah's Messenger ﷺ. The *Mujaddid* surmised from this man's acrimonious expression that he was a crypto-Wahhābī, and upon further investigation it was discovered that he was a disciple (*Murīd*) of Rashīd Ahmad Gangohī, the founder of an Islamic seminary in Deoband (India) that is heavily influence by the deviant Wahhābī /"Salafī" sect. From that time on, Imām Ahmad began to deliver lectures in refutation to the erroneous beliefs of the Wahhābīyyah. Rashīd Ahmad's disciple sat through one more lecture, and never attended another discourse by the Imām again. A'lā Hazrat ؓ thanked Allah for purifying his sanctified assembly (*Majlis*)![212]

Several members of Imām Ahmad's Hajj group started experiencing sharp stomach pains just as the period of quarantine was ending. Mawlānā Muhammad Razā ؓ asked his elder brother what they should do, because the doctors would be there any minute. A'lā Hazrat ؓ pointed out that it would be a terrible misfortune to miss the rites of Hajj on account of a bout of stomach flu. As time was of the essence their group agreed to observe silence on the matter. By way of reassurance Imām Ahmad said, "Please give me a moment, dear brother, to consult my personal

---

[212] Imām Mustafā Razā Khān, *al-Malfūz al-Sharīf*, 2:163-164.

physician (al-Ghawth al-A'zam ﷺ)." With these mysterious words he left the compound and walked to an uninhabited area of land, and began to recite the supplications given to us by the Revered One ﷺ in the Hadīth Sharīf. He also turned to the Chieftain of the Saints, Sayyidunā ash-Shaykh Muhyi'd-dīn 'Abdul Qādir al-Jīlānī ﷺ, as a means of approach (*Wasīla*), since the Ghawth is empowerd by Allah to bring succor to humanity in times of extreme adversity. All of a sudden a direct descendent of Shaykh 'Abdul Qādir ﷺ, Hazrat Ghūlām Jīlānī ﷺ of Bansa Sharīf, was standing before the Imām. They had boarded the ship together in Mumbai; and his inexplicable appearance marked the acceptance of A'lā Hazrat's supplication. Imām Ahmad ﷺ asked Hazrat Ghūlām Jīlānī ﷺ to offer prayers and supplications for the welfare of his group which the venerable saint did. When A'lā Hazrat returned to camp, some ten minutes later, he discovered that everyone was in the pink of health, as if they had never even felt a tinge of pain or discomfort by the grace of Allah Most Pure![213]

There was a massive gathering of pilgrims in Jeddah; and Imām Ahmad's stately group was among them. The Hajj

---

[213] Imām Mustafā Razā Khān, *al-Malfūz al-Sharīf*, 2:164.

Regard for Women

authorities made everyone walk in a single file line to an immigration camp. But the pilgrims were expected to stand in the scorching sun with no protection or provisions whatsoever, and the women were feeling extremely fatigued. Their line was barely moving and they had been waiting for five hours in the blistering midday heat! Morale was low and many of the pilgrims were becoming more and more frustrated with the situation. At last Mawlānā Muhammad Razā ؓ and Shaykh Hāmid ؓ approached A'lā Hazrat ؓ saying, "How long are we to languish in this stifling heat without food or drink?" The Imām replied, "If you are in a hurry, then by all means go ahead of us. But I will not leave until the crowd disperses, because it is impossible to escort the women through this horde." Everyone heeded Imām Ahmad's good counsel and appreciated his regard for the safety and welfare of their sisters. This, of course, is the second incident in the midst of A'lā Hazrat's Pilgrimage that tells us of his personal gallantry. To the believing men and women he was like a chivalrous knight inspired by the Sunnah of our liege-lord, the king of Allah's creation,[214] Sayyidunā Muhammad ﷺ.[215]

---

[214] For further discussion of the kingship and authority granted to the Prophet ﷺ by Allah Most Pure, see Muftī Ahmed Yār Khān Na'īmi Ashrafī's *The Holy Prophet's Kingdom* ﷺ, and Shaykh 'Abdul Hādī's *The Authority of Prophet Muhammad* ﷺ *in the Kingdom of Allah* ﷻ (DVD).
[215] Imām Mustafā Razā Khān, *al-Malfūz al-Sharīf*, 2:164-165.

The *Hujjāj* waited in silence hoping against hope that the line would move. After some time a stranger of Arab ancestry greeted the *Mujaddid* and inquired, "O Shaykh! What seems to be the matter?" A'lā Hazrat ﷺ answered, "The problem is obvious [to anyone]; we have been standing in this heat for over five hours with our sisters, and the crowd has no foreseeable end." The Arab man then told their group to form a circle with the men on the outside and the women in the center. They followed the stranger through the massive gathering of people. Their shoulders did not brush against a single pilgrim. Once they were out of the crowd the Arab man vanished right before their very eyes. Shaykh 'Abdul Hādī notes in his English translation of *al-Malfūz al-Sharīf* [The Noble Vocals] that the stranger was none other than Sayyidunā Khidr ﷺ, who came incognito to aid the *Mujaddid* of this Umma.[216] All praise belongs to Allah alone, who works in mysterious ways! In the words of the Epistle to the Romans: *O, the depth of the riches both of the wisdom and knowledge of God! How unsearchable are His judgments and His ways past finding out!*[217]

As the pilgrims were passing through the city of Jeddah, Al'ā Hazrat ﷺ was smitten with a raging fever that caused his whole body to chill. He entered the state of

---

[216] Imām Mustafā Razā Khān, *al-Malfūz al-Sharīf*, 2:165.
[217] 11:33.

consecration (*Ihrām*) when they arrived at the assembly point designated by the Sacred Law (*Mīqāt Sharī'ah*) for people coming from the East (*Dhāt 'Irq*). Since it is impermissible to cover the head and face in *Ihrām*, Imām Ahmad ؎ wrapped his body up to the neck and went to sleep. He praised Allah the Exalted upon waking for his head remained uncovered whilst he was sleeping! Alas and alack, his fever increased during their three-day stay in Jeddah. To make matters worse, the pilgrims had to spend the night in an open field; and the cool night air seemed to exacerbate Imām Ahmad's condition. He pleaded to the Prophet ؎, who was sent by Allah as a mercy to the worlds, for healing (*Shifā*), and asked that he might undertake this Pilgrimage in good health. A'lā Hazrat ؎ was cured instantly; and he felt profound gratitude toward the One who had lifted his fever, so much so that after the 13th day of *Dhu'l-Hijja* he exclaimed, "Now I do not care if I get fever again, because the Most Merciful Lord has answered my prayers." Lo and behold, his fever did not return until the month of Hajj had nearly reached its end.[218]

One of the most important virtues that we can acquire from the life of A'lā Hazrat ؎ is absolute trust in the Lord (*Tawakkul*). Whenever and wherever an obstacle would rear its ugly head, he would devote himself totally to

---

[218] Imām Mustafā Razā Khān, *al-Malfūz al-Sharīf*, 2:165-166.

Reflections of Allah's Love

Allah Almighty, and turn his attention away from all those who were beneath Him. It may be said that Imām Ahmad had reached the stage of delegation (*Sāhib at-Tafwīd*) and was happy to accept the decree (*Hukm*) of his Lord. The general guidance on this subject is contained in His words: *And when someone puts all his trust in Allah, He will be enough for him*.[219] *And put all your trust [in Allah], if you are indeed believers*.[220] By way of comparison, the common folk (*'Awāmm*) have a habit of looking at secondary causes first and then we like to take our complaints to the creation. Whereas, the elite (*Khawāss*) and the elite of the elite (*Khawāss al-Khawāss*) turn toward the Creator of the heavens and the earth, and are utterly content to rely upon His judgement and decree.

Imām Ahmad ﷺ completed the rites of Pilgrimage and went straight to the Library of the Meccan Sanctuary. There he and his noble son, Shaykh Hāmid, had the pleasure of meeting Sayyid Ismā'īl Effendī ﷺ, one of the foremost scholars in the ennobled city of Mecca, who was blessed with a dashing personality. Although Sayyid Ismā'īl ﷺ was unacquainted with A'lā Hazrat personally,

---

[219] Al-Qur'ān, 65:3.
[220] Al-Qur'ān, 5:23.

he like other great 'Ulamā of Mecca was no stranger to his name. This was their first encounter, but Sayyid Ismā'īl ﷺ had read Imām Ahmad's *Fatāwā al-Haramayn bi Rajf Nadwat al-Mayn* [Edicts of the Sacred Sanctuaries shaking the lying council]. The august *Mujaddid* wrote this doctrinal treatise in less than twenty hours, and sent it to scholars and muftīs of the Haramayn to authenticate and endorse in 1316/1900. Sixteen Meccan scholars wrote commendations for this work. They also conferred many titles upon its author. From that time forward Sunni scholars from the Arab world held A'lā Hazrat ﷺ in great regard and respect.[221]

Sayyid Ismā'īl ﷺ was engrossed in his research when someone in the library asked him a question about one of the duties of Hajj. The questioner wanted to know about the legality of throwing stones against the pillars before noon (*Zawāl*). Sayyid Ismā'īl ﷺ answered by saying, "The scholars of Mecca have ruled that it is permissible." But Shaykh Hāmid ﷺ objected and began to discuss the matter with him. When A'lā Hazrat ﷺ was asked his opinion, he said, "To throw stones against the pillars before noon is contrary to the laws of Hajj in the Hanafī school." Sayyid Ismā'īl ﷺ quoted a famous book of Islamic jurisprudence and replied, "Its permissibility is mentioned in that book; and there is consensus." Imām Ahmad reflected upon his

---

[221] Imām Mustafā Razā Khān, *al-Malfūz al-Sharīf*, 2:166.

words and said, "The legality may be mentioned in that book,[222] but there is no consensus on this issue." Sayyid Ismā'īl ؓ found the book in question and opened it. All praise belongs to Allah alone, it was as A'lā Hazrat said! The noble Sayyid discreetly asked Shaykh Hāmid, "Who is this man?" Upon hearing the Imām's name, Sayyid Ismā'īl ؓ rose to his feet and held A'lā Hazrat ؓ in a tight embrace. Henceforward, both men shared a strong bond of love and admiration for each other.[223]

There was a divine purpose behind Imām Ahmad's Pilgrimage that the Most Just of all judges in His infinite wisdom was about to divulge. The crypto-Wahhābīs had arrived in Mecca before A'lā Hazrat ؓ and the Deobandī scholar, Khalīl Ahmad Sahāranpūrī (d. 1346/1927),[224] was among them. The scholars of Deoband had perpetuated Wahhābīsm in South Asia for the better part of nineteen years.[225] They sought to "purify" the religion and the Hanafī school in particular from what they perceived as

---

[222] To cast stones before noon on the 11th and 12th days of Hajj will render this rite null and void. In consequence, a penalty sacrifice (*Dam*) will be necessary. It is somewhat disliked (*Makrūh Tahzīhī*) to do so on the 13th day. If stones are cast before noon on this day, then a penalty sacrifice is not required. For further discussion of this topic, see *al-Fatāwā al-Ridāwiyyah*, 10:754.

[223] Imām Mustafā Razā Khān, *al-Malfūz al-Sharīf*, 2:166-167.

[224] Sahāranpūrī was also widely known as Khalīl Ahmad Ambhetwī.

[225] Imām Ahmad Razā Khān, "Tamheedul-Īmān" in *Thesis of Imam Ahmad Raza* (Durban: Barkātur-Razā Publications, 2005), trans. Shaykh 'Abdul Hādī, 4:132-136.

Regard for Women

polytheistic innovations and false beliefs. Some of their books such as *Tahzīr al-Nās, Āb al-Hayāt, Tasfiyat al-'Aqā'id, Tazkirat ar-Rashīd, Fatāwā Rashīdiyya, al-Barāhīn al-Qāti'a, Hifz al-Īmān, Risālah al-Imdād*, and *Tafsīr Bulghatul Hayrān* contain passages that constitute clear disparagement of our Master, Prophet Muhammad ﷺ.[226] It goes without saying that when Muslims try to demean the station and honor of Allah's Beloved Prophet ﷺ under the guise of refuting innovation (*Bid'ah*), "defending Islam against *Shirk*,"[227] or modernism, it is beyond irreverent and enters the realm of the heretical. The great tragedy in this is that in the name of "pure" monotheism (*Tawhīd*), people in British India (who claimed to be Sunni Hanafīs, Sufis, Ash'arīs or Māturīdīs[228]) began to disrespect the Prophet ﷺ.

A'lā Hazrat ﷺ wrote a myriad of refutations to such aberrant doctrines. But when the fullness of time had come, he issued a *Fatwā* against the Deobandī shaykhs, and deemed them non-Muslims (*Kāfirs*) and apostates (*Murtadd*) for maliciously insulting Allah and His

---

[226] Imām Ahmad Razā Khān, "Tamheedul-Īmān" in *Thesis of Imam Ahmad Raza*, 4:153.

[227] *Shirk*: Associating partners with Allah Most Pure.

[228] Those that follow one of the two orthodox schools of Islamic doctrine in Sunni Islam are known as Ash'arīs or Māturīdīs. These theological schools were named after their respective founders, Shaykh Abu'l-Hasan al-Ash'arī ﷺ and Shaykh Abū Mansūr Muhammad al-Māturīdī ﷺ.

Reflections of Allah's Love

Messenger ﷺ. This *Fatwā*, entitled *Al-Mu'tamad al-Mustanad* [The Reliable Proofs], was first published in the Subcontinent in 1320/1902. However, the scholars of Deoband remained callous and unrepentant due to their unwavering faith in certain fanciful heresies like *Imkān al-Kidhb*[229] or the possibility of [Allah's] lying as well as their notorious allegation that the Prophet ﷺ "was not aware of his ultimate fate and of things beyond a wall."[230] Their devilry went so far as to charge Sunni Muslims with idolatry (*Shirk*) for believing in the Prophet's knowledge of the unseen ﷺ. Yet Khalīl Ahmad speciously affirmed this same type of knowledge for Satan the accursed in his *al-Barāhīn al-Qāti'a*, which Rashīd Ahmad Gangohī endorsed and eulogized.[231] Khalīl Ahmad practiced concealment (*Taqiyyah*) to hide his views from the Haramayn 'Ulamā,[232]

---

[229] *Kidhb* is an Arabic word meaning: (1) lie, (2) lying, (3) falsehood, etc. (The form *Kadhib*, which the reader may come across elsewhere, is simply an alternative transliteration of the Arabic spelling. South Asian Muslims tend to use the form *Kizb* by substituting –z for –dh.)

[230] Khalīl Ahmad in his *Barāhīn al-Qāti'a* attributed this forged narration to Shaykh 'Abdul Haqq ﷺ, but the latter had clearly stated that it was unauthentic. Nuh Keller is probably the first contemporary scholar to forward Khalīl Ahmad's inaccurate attribution in his controversial Deobandī apologetic "Iman, Kufr, and Takfir." Keller himself admits in endnote 29 that he was unable to identify a credible reference for this citation.

[231] For further discussion of this topic, see Maryam Qadri, *The Voice of Truth*.

[232] Khalīl Ahmad continued to practice concealment (*Taqiyyah*) even after being exposed and condemned by the Haramayn 'Ulamā (*al-*

Regard for Women

but that did not prevent him from contesting the amount of unseen knowledge that the Prophet ﷺ was given, nor did it dissuade him from attempting to condemn a Sunni scholar from India.

To this end, Khalīl Aḥmad had obtained access to the ministers of Mecca, right up to the Sharīf and raised certain questions about the Prophet's knowledge of the unseen ﷺ to a scholar of great standing in the Ḥanafī school, Shaykh ash-Sayyid Ṣāliḥ Kamāl ؓ. The Deobandī shaykh attempted to charge Mawlānā Salāmatu'llāh ؓ (from Rampur) with disbelief (*Takfīr*) for holding that the Prophet ﷺ had immense knowledge of the unseen. When Imām Aḥmad came to know of this unfortunate turn of events, he hastened to meet with Shaykh ash-Sayyid Ṣāliḥ Kamāl ؓ. The *Mujaddid* was accompanied by Mawlānā 'Abdul Ahad son of 'Allāma Wasi Ahmad Muhaddith ؓ (from Surt).[233]

After initiating the *salām* and shaking hands, Imām Aḥmad spoke for two hours to Shaykh ash-Sayyid Ṣāliḥ about the unseen (*Ghayb*), and the scope of prophetic knowledge (*'Ilm*). He supported each and every statement with definitive proofs from the Holy Qur'ān, Ḥadīth

---

Malfūz al-Sharīf, 2:177-180). Ultimately the Deobandī shaykh had to flee the ennobled city of Mecca for Jeddah, because the People of the Sunnah objected to his visit.

[233] Imām Muṣṭafā Razā Khān, *al-Malfūz al-Sharīf*, 2:167. Surt, also known as Sirt or Sirte, is a city in Libya.

Sharīf, and the opinions of the scholastic theologians and jurists of mainstream Sunni Islam. In addition to this, he accurately presented the view of the Wahhābī sect and refuted all of their false claims with exquisite clarity and penetrating insight. Shaykh ash-Sayyid Sālih listened attentively to A'lā Hazrat's discourse. Once it was over, he rose from his seat, went to a cabinet and picked up a paper. He had recorded some questions on the same subject that were posed to Mawlānā Salamatu'llāh ﷺ. A few questions had remained blank and were not properly or fully answered. The venerable Sayyid handed this document to Imām Ahmad and said, "Your arrival in Mecca is a mercy from Allah the Exalted, because I surely would have dispatched a verdict of disbelief against Mawlānā Salamatu'llāh ﷺ if you had not come today." A'lā Hazrat ﷺ gave thanks and exaltation to the One who grants success and returned to his hostel! Shaykh ash-Sayyid Sālih hoped to meet Imām Ahmad again and looked for him in the Library of the Meccan Sanctuary.[234]

Gratitude (*Shukr*) is one of the central themes in Imām Ahmad's life, in every moment he was acknowledging the benefaction of the Benefactor, with an attitude of humility, for the Exalted has said: *If you are thankful, I will surely give you more; but if you are ungrateful, My punishment is terrible*

---

[234] Imām Mustafā Razā Khān, *al-Malfūz al-Sharīf*, 2:167-168.

Regard for Women

indeed.²³⁵ Our Prophet ﷺ was a thankful servant (*'Abdul Shakūr*) and he has told us that: **"The first of those to enter the Garden of Paradise will be those who are constantly praising Allah [*al-hammādūna li'llāh*].**"²³⁶ Thankfulness (*Shukr*) is the lifeblood of a believer; therefore, we should endeavor to increase our praise of the Lord, for He has promised us in a holy utterance (*Hadīth Qudsī*) narrated on the authority of al-Bukhārī and Muslim that: **"I am to my servant as he expects of Me, I am with him when he remembers Me. If he remembers Me in his heart, I remember him to Myself, and if he remembers me in an assembly, I mention him in an assembly better than his."**²³⁷ For further discussion of this topic, see Sayyidunā ash-Shaykh Muhyi'd-dīn 'Abdul Qādir al-Jīlānī's *Sufficient Provision for Seekers of the Path of Truth*, 5:132-139.

A'lā Hazrat ؓ returned to the Library of the Meccan Sanctuary on the 25ᵗʰ of *Dhu'l-Hijja*. There he met with numerous scholars, including Shaykh ash-Sayyid Sālih ؓ, Shaykh ash-Sayyid Ismā'īl Effendī ؓ, his father, Shaykh ash-Sayyid Khalīl ؓ, and his brother, Shaykh ash-Sayyid Mustafā ؓ. The Friends of Allah Most High asked Imām

---

²³⁵ Al-Qur'ān, 14:7.
²³⁶ Shaykh 'Abdul Qādir al-Jīlānī, *Sufficient Provision for Seekers of the Path of Truth* (Hollywood: Al-Baz Publishing, Inc., 1997), trans. Muhtar Holland, 5:138.
²³⁷ Related on the authority of al-Bukhārī and Muslim.

Reflections of Allah's Love

Ahmad to answer five questions concerning knowledge of the unseen that were given to them by the Wahhābīyyah. His response would then be presented to the Sharīf of the ennobled city of Mecca. These great dignitaries beseeched the *Mujaddid* to silence the Wahhābīs forever; but he only had two days to write a reply. Trusting in the grace of Allah and the succor of His Messenger ﷺ, Imām Ahmad agreed to complete the task within the allotted timeframe.[238]

Look at the glory of the All-Majestic Lord, who afflicted His servant with another ragging fever,[239] yet

---

[238] Imām Mustafā Razā Khān, *al-Malfūz al-Sharīf*, 2:168-169.

[239] Imām Ahmad ؓ commented upon the spiritual significance of headaches and fevers in his *al-Malfūz al-Sharīf* saying: "Headaches and fevers are blessed ailments, which were experienced by all the Prophets of Allah. Once a Friend of Allah had a headache and yet he was overjoyed, as the Bountiful Lord had blessed him with an ailment of the Prophets. He then spent the entire night engrossed in supererogatory prayers to thank Allah for this mercy. Allah is the Greatest (*Allahu Akbar*)! But alas, today, if someone gets a mild headache then he wants to perform his ritual prayer quickly and sometimes he even abstains from it. The rule is that pain becomes an expiation of our sins (*Kaffara*) for that specific part of the body that is afflicted. This is not so in the case of fever, because this particular ailment penetrates the entire body and therefore, fever is a *Kaffara* for the sins of the entire body. Indeed, this is a great blessing of Allah Almighty upon our Community. This ailment actually cleanses one of sins. All praise belongs to Allah alone (*Alhamdulillāh*)! The Exalted Lord has been exceptionally merciful to me because I often experience both of these Prophetic ailments" (1:80). When the Prophets of Allah experienced headaches and fevers it was not to expiate their sins, as they are sinless, rather they took the sins of

Regard for Women

enabled him to complete the task at hand! A'lā Hazrat ﷺ decided not to write about "the five [unseen] things" mentioned at the end of Sūrah Luqman (31:34), because the Wahhābīs did not mention it in their questions. But whilst he was feverishly working, he received a message from the Preceptor (*Ustād*) of the 'Ulamā, Shaykh Ahmad Abul Khair Mirdād ﷺ, who said, "Paralysis has kept me from meeting you, yet I am very eager to hear your answer!" A'lā Hazrat hastened to Shaykh Ahmad's bedside with the first chapter of his treatise. He was busy writing the second chapter, when the *Ustād al-'Ulamā* asked him to include something about the five unseen things as well. With utmost respect the Imām agreed to acquiescent his request and gently touched his foot as a mark of *Ādāb*. Although Shaykh Ahmad ﷺ was an elder of Mecca and a very accomplished scholar well over seventy years of age, he looked to A'lā Hazrat ﷺ and said, "I kiss your feet, and I kiss your sandals!" Verily his exclamation was a mercy and blessing from the Messenger of Allah ﷺ. To be honored by a senior scholar of Shaykh Ahmad's caliber was a tremendous boon for this meek servant of the Chosen One ﷺ (*'Abdul Mustafā* ﷺ).[240]

---

their own communities upon themselves and expiated them in this way. And Allah knows best.
[240] Imām Mustafā Razā Khān, *al-Malfūz al-Sharīf*, 2:169-170.

Imām Ahmad ﷺ completed his celebrated *ad-Dawlah al-Makkiyyah bi'l Māddati'l Ghaybiyyah* [The Meccan Treasure on the Matter of the Unseen] after the evening prayer (*'Ishā*) on the following day, and sent it to Shaykh ash-Sayyid Sālih ﷺ. This book was an overnight sensation. In fact, the Sharīf ﷺ of Mecca would not part with it! Seventy-seven scholars from the Hijaz, Yemen, Syria, and Egypt embellished *ad-Dawlah al-Makkiyyah* with fantastic commentaries that extolled its author, who won widespread acclaim. It has become a modern classic, for example, Shaykh Sayyid Abu'l Hudā Muhammad al-Yaqūbī ash-Shadhilī said that he read it twice; and benefited from it a lot, and that it is "one of the best works on this subject."[241] In much the same vein, Shaykh Gibril Fouad Haddad in *Albani & His Friends: A Concise Guide to the Salafi Movement* said that the Imām offered "the greatest and most definitive answers on this chapter."[242] In a single blow A'lā Hazrat Mujaddid Imām Ahmad Razā Khān al-Qādirī ﷺ crushed the false claims made by the

---

[241] This remark was made during a live *Takbeer TV* interview that aired on the 21st of Rajab 1431, which corresponds to July 3, 2010. One may view the segment on Imām Ahmad Razā Khān al-Qādirī by visiting http://www.youtube.com/watch?v=b92u3Rh7oUc.

[242] Shaykh Monawwar Ateeq, "Knowledge of the Unseen Theology: Arguments on the Scope of Prophetic Knowledge,"accessed on April 19, 2012, http://scholarsink.files.wordpress.com/2011/06/knowledge oftheunseentheology.pdf, 9.

Regard for Women

Wahhābīyyah and proved that Sayyidunā Muhammad ﷺ had knowledge of the unseen and that it was immense knowledge of the past and future such that no other Prophet or creature was granted. He also saved a fellow Muslim from the charge of disbelief in the process. *Allah will choose for His special Mercy whom He will, for Allah is Lord of grace abounding.*[243]

It should come as no surprise that after this incident Imām Ahmad ؓ decided to present the blasphemous statements penned by the scholars of Deoband to the illustrious 'Ulamā of the Meccan and Medinan Sanctuaries. Thus his *Fatwā* condemning the Deobandīs, entitled *al-Mu'tamad al-Mustanad* [The Reliable Proofs], was sent to the highest echelons of Sunni law for authentication. Thirty-three scholars from three of the four juristic schools of Sunni law (namely the Hanafī, Shāfi'ī, and Mālikī) endorsed this *Fatwā*. Their praise, commendation, and edicts were compiled into one famous book, *Husām al-Haramayn 'alā Manhar al-Kufr wa al-Mayn* [The Sword of the Sacred Sanctuaries on the Slaughter Point of Blasphemy and Falsehood].[244] The staunch support of the Meccan and

---

[243] Al-Qur'ān 2:105.
[244] Sanyal, *Ahmad Riza Khan Barelwi*, 108-109.

Medinan scholars forced the Deobandīs to repudiate their odious beliefs, which heretofore had proceeded unabated. Khalīl Ahmad left the Hoy City two weeks after his arrival in utter disgrace, and was compelled to write an official book on *'Aqīdah* to get their school reinstated.[245] What else could the Deobandīs do when confronted by the knights of the Messenger's army ﷺ, who strengthened Imām Ahmad's *Fatwā* with their support, and came to the aid of the Prophet's religion ﷺ? As the most learned scholar from Egypt, Imām Abū Ja'far al-Warrāq at-Tahāwī ﷺ (d. 321/933), said in his reliable articulation of Muslim belief, "All things are in accordance with His determination and will, and His will is fulfilled."[246]

Prior to this historic event, the Deobandīs had spent the better part of their academic careers defending and upholding their books of unsound doctrine, in which, they had blasphemed (*Kafara*) against the Lord of Truth and

---

[245] Khalīl Ahmad repudiated their blasphemous statements in his *al-Muhannad 'alā al-Mufannad* [The Sword on the Disapproved]. Although sound, this book is problematic on a number of levels, primarily because the scholars of Deoband did not recant fully by admitting that they once held heterodox views. Instead they chose to deny penning their decisive statements of disbelief. For more than a century, Deobandī authorities have continued to promulgate their books of unsound doctrine like *Tahzīr al-Nās*, *Fatāwā Rashīdiyya*, *al-Barāhīn al-Qāti'a*, *Hifz al-Īmān*, etc. which casts a shadow on their Sunni creed, and causes many to question its authenticity.

[246] Imām at-Tahāwī's quote was excerpted from *The Creed of Imam al-Tahāwī* (Berkeley: Zaytuna Institute, 2007), 52.

Regard for Women

His Messenger ﷺ. These dubious scholars took pride in their malicious beliefs, which is why they attempted to desecrate the Holy House in the sanctified month of Hajj by charging an innocent Sunni scholar with disbelief (*Takfīr*) and by raising audacious questions about the Prophet's knowledge of the unseen ﷺ. Allah debased them for their wickedness and raised the honor of His sincere servant from Bareilly. In the wise words attributed to Prophet Sulaymān ﷺ in the Book of Proverbs: *Pride goeth before destruction and a haughty spirit before the fall.*[247] *But humility comes before honor.*[248]

The guardians of the Prophetic Sunnah in Mecca wanted A'lā Hazrat ﷺ to extend his stay with them. They even offered to find him a second wife. But he very sweetly declined their proposal by saying: "My wife is a humble slave of Allah, and I have brought her here to perform the Pilgrimage.[249] Does she deserve to be disheartened on my account?"[250] He denied his own rights out of regard for Sayyidah Irshād Begum ﷺ, which brings us to our final anecdote in this chapter of his venerable

---

[247] 16:18.
[248] 18:12.
[249] In all probability, A'lā Hazrat ﷺ gave Sayyidah Irshād Begum ﷺ permission to embark on her Pilgrimage with a *Mahram* (unmarriable kin) which would explain why she is not mentioned at the beginning of his trip from Bareilly to Mumbai.
[250] Imām Mustafā Razā Khān, *al-Malfūz al-Sharīf*, 2:192.

life. See how beautifully Imām Ahmad ﷺ adhered to our Prophet's ﷺ words: **"The believer with the most perfect faith is the one who has the best character and the one who is kindest to his wife."**[251] Please turn to volume two of *al-Malfūz al-Sharīf* [The Noble Vocals] to learn about A'lā Hazrat's visitation to the illumined city of Medina and his activities there.

---

[251] Mawlānā 'Abdul-Alīm Siddiquī al-Qādirī, "Women and Their Status in Islam" in *Dimensions of Islam* (Durban: Barkātur-Razā Publications, 2005), 205.

A Red-Letter Day

For the devoted followers of Sayyidunā ash-Shaykh Muhyi'd-dīn 'Abdul Qādir al-Jīlānī al-Hasanī al-Husainī ؓ (d. 561/1166) the 10th of Rabī' al-Ākhir is a day of tremendous thanksgiving and anticipation,[252] because it marks the beginning of the *Ghiyarwī Sharīf* (or, the anniversary of Shaykh 'Abdul Qādir al-Jīlānī's ؓ union with the Beloved), which is customarily held, around the world, on the 11th of Rabī' al-Ākhir. *Ghiyarwī* is an Urdu word that literally means "eleven." On this virtuous day in the year 1325 AH (May 23, 1907), those in the Razā household were doubly blessed, for the coolness of their eyes, the saviour of the Umma, the voice of A'lā Hazrat ؓ, the legend of his age, the beloved Friend (*Walī*) of Allah, the sea of direct knowledge *(Ma'rifa)* and reality *(Haqīqah)*, the outstanding exegete, and the first lotus blossom from

---

[252] As the author's honorable Murshid al-Kāmil (may Allah sanctify his lofty secret and grant him a long life) says: "If a merchant of peppers can count on his wares for a profit, will the one who reposes faith in the supreme Ghawth ؓ be left empty-handed? Allah forbid! Not in this world and certainly not in the hereafter."

the garden of Hujjat al-Islām ﷺ, Shaykh Muhammad Ibrāhīm Razā Khān al-Qādirī ﷺ, was born in the city of Bareilly.[253]

In accordance with the Sunnah, the *Adhān* was recited in the right ear of the newborn and the *Iqāmah* in his left. Imām Ahmad ﷺ chewed a piece of date and placed it into the mouth of baby Ibrāhīm (*Tahnīk*).[254] His great-uncle, *Ustād al-Zamān* (or, "The Preceptor of the Time") Shaykh Hasan Razā Khān al-Qādirī ﷺ, waxed lyrical at the moment of his grandnephew's birth and recited a Persian couplet to mark the occasion:

May knowledge and life and good fortune [be yours little child] by the Grace of the Exalted One.[255]

A'lā Hazrat's ﷺ mood was expansive on this jubilant occasion and he had new clothes stitched for his relatives, close friends, students, and spiritual successors. Muftī

---

[253] The author wishes to thank Mawlānā Muhammad Kalīm al-Qādirī for giving her permission to utilize his unpublished biography on the life of Shaykh Ibrāhīm Razā Khān ﷺ. Most, if not all, of this chapter is taken from his manuscript.

[254] It is established from the Ahādīth that the Companions took newborns to the Prophet Muhammad ﷺ for *Tahnīk*, and he would chew something sweet like dates and place it in the baby's palate. *Tahnīk* is a preferable practice from the Sunnah that is usually performed by a pious member of the household.

[255] The numerical value of this impromptu poem corresponds to the year of the baby's birth, 1325 AH (*Tadhkira al-'Ulamā Ahl Sunnat*, 56).

A Red-Letter Day

Muhammad Zafar ad-Dīn Bihārī ﷺ, was among those in attendance and commented upon it in his *Hayāt-e A'lā Hazrat* [The Life of A'lā Hazrat]:

"After the birth of his newborn grandson and in accordance with the ruling of the Sacred Law, A'lā Hazrat Imām Ahmad Razā Khān al-Qādirī ﷺ slaughtered an animal on behalf of the child (*'Aqīqa*) and prepared a grand feast. However, this was such a blissful event for the family that it was done with great pomp and circumstance. Along with friends and relations [of the Razā household], all the students studying at Dār al-'Ulūm Manzar al-Islām were invited to attend the ceremony. The cook was given special instructions to prepare each dish according to the student's acquired taste. Thus, [mouth-watering] African cuisine was prepared for the African students, [succulent] Indian food for the Indians, and [tasty] Afganī dishes were served to students from Afghanistan such as large flat bread and [savory, spicy] meat stewed to perfection. Indian students from the states of Bihar and Uttar Pradesh were served two types of rice pilaf with korma—a mildly spiced meat dish in a cream or yogurt sauce. Likewise, [delightfully delicious] fish was prepared with a side of rice for the Bengalī students. Verily, this extraordinary feast was one of a kind. The august *Mujaddid*, A'lā Hazrat Imām Ahmad Razā Khān al-Qādirī ﷺ, supervised the entire function [from beginning to end with meticulous care]."[256]

It was a tradition in the Razā household to commence the Islamic education of children at the age of four years, four months, and four days. Throughout the lands of Islam, Muslim children inaugurate their study of Sacred Knowledge by reciting the Name of Allah. This act of consecration is customarily known as the *"Bismi'llāh* ceremony," and little Ibrāhīm ﷺ had the singular honor of invoking the Name of Allah under the supervision of his paternal grandfather (Imām Ahmad Razā Khān ﷺ) in the presence of notable personalities of the city, including great Sufi saints (*'Awliyā*) and authoritative scholars (*'Ulamā*). Sweets were then distributed to all those present.

In the midst of this prestigious gathering that took place on the 14th of Sha'bān in the year 1329/1911, A'lā Hazrat ﷺ made his beloved grandson a disciple (*Murīd*) blessing the youth with spiritual successorship (*Khalīfah*), as well as authorization (*Ijāzat*) in all of the Sufi orders transmitted to him through his noble *Mashā'ikh*. Imām

---

[256] Shaykh al-Muftī 'Abdul Wajid al-Qādirī, *Hayāt-e Mufassir-e A'zam Hind* (Delhi: Al-Qur'ān Islamic Foundation, 2003), 10.

A Red-Letter Day

Ahmad ؓ acted as an agent (*Wakīl*) on behalf of his son, Shaykh Hāmid ؓ, who was his principle successor (*Sajjād Nashin*).[257] Thus, Shaykh Ibrāhīm's line of transmission passes first through his beloved father and then onto A'lā Hazrat ؓ.

Some of those present were baffled by this divine grant, for they had never seen a youth of four blessed with *Ijāzat* and *Khalīfah*. Nevertheless, their regard for Imām Ahmad ؓ was such that they remained wonderstruck in his presence. Through his penetrating spiritual insight, A'lā Hazrat ؓ was made aware of their inner thoughts and feelings, so he proclaimed to all those in attendance: "O People! One day this grandson of mine shall become my [foremost] spokesman!"

In after years the Bountiful Lord opened everyone's eyes to the miraculous powers (*Karāmāt*) of A'lā Hazrat ؓ, for within a quarter of a century Shaykh Ibrāhīm ؓ grew to be an indefatigable crusader of Islam aiding the Community through his written works, legendary orations, and finesse in the classroom. Everyone had to admit that this great man of Allah was not only a peerless commentator of the Holy Qur'ān, master of the Hadīth sciences, an adept metaphysician (*Murshid*), and gifted orator, but also the "voice" of A'lā Hazrat ؓ. In point of

---

[257] *Sajjād Nashin*: One of the foremost deputies of a Murshid and the keeper of his Sufi center (*Khānqah*).

fact, numerous people have narrated that after listening to Shaykh Ibrāhīm's commentary of the glorious Qur'ān, or his contextualization and corresponding explanation of a Hadīth, the listener felt as though he was hearing the said Qur'ānic verse or Hadīth of Allah's beloved Messenger ﷺ for the very first time![258]

Shaykh Ibrāhīm ؓ was the coolness of the family's eyes and their center of hope and aspiration; his initial education and upbringing (*Tarbiyyah*) was carefully supervised at home under the benevolent tutorship of his noble mother and paternal grandmother (Sayyidah Irshād Begum), who taught him how to recite the entire Holy Qur'ān and introduced him to the nuances of the Urdu language which enabled him to speak and write eloquently in one of the major mother tongues of South Asia.

When Shaykh Ibrāhīm ؓ reached the age of seven he began to study at the Dār al-'Ulūm Manzar al-Islām in Bareilly. Although the Islamic seminary was only ten years old, it was home to some very prestigious exoteric and esoteric scholars such as Shāms al-'Ulamā Rahm-e Ilahi Muzaffarnagarī ؓ, Mawlānā Zuhur al-Hasan al-Faruqī Rampurī ؓ, Sadr ash-Sharī'ah[259] Shaykh Amjad

---

[258] Shaykh al-Muftī 'Abdul Wajid al-Qādirī, *Hayāt-e Mufassir-e A'zam Hind*, 34-35.
[259] *Sadr ash-Sharī'ah*: "The Chief Islamicist."

A Red-Letter Day

'Alī al-A'zmī ؑ, and Mawlānā Nūr al-Husain Mujaddid ؑ. There were also some teachers who had graduated from the Dār al-'Ulūm itself and had now started teaching in it like Shaykh Mustafā Razā Khān al-Qādirī ؑ, Shaykh Hasanain Razā Khān al-Qādirī ؑ, and Mawlānā Ihsan 'Alī Muzaffarpurī ؑ. The latter once told the Grand Muftī of Holland, 'Abdul Wajid, that: "I taught Jīlānī Miyān[260] *Kafiya, Fusul Akbari, Quduri*, etc. but I esteem him as I respect my own spiritual mentor, Hujjat al-Islām Shaykh Hāmid Razā Khān."[261]

Shaykh Ibrāhīm ؑ completed the intermediate and advanced books of Sacred Knowledge under the tutorship of Mawlānā Ihsan 'Alī Sahīb Muhaddith Faidpurī Bihārī ؑ. For instance, he read *al-Kafiyah* in Arabic etymology, *al-Quduri* in Islamic jurisprudence, and *Fusul Akbari* in logic. His venerable father ؑ taught him classical Arabic and acquainted him with the literature of the Arabs; Shaykh Hāmid also instructed him in 'Allāma at-Tabrīzī's renowned Hadīth compilation *Mishkāt al-Masābīh* taking him to the pinnacle of Sacred Knowledge.[262]

---

[260] Shaykh Ibrāhīm's ؑ paternal grandmother affectionately referred to him as "Jīlānī Miyān," as did many of those who held him in great regard and respect.
[261] Shaykh al-Muftī 'Abdul Wajid al-Qādirī, *Hayāt-e Mufassir-e A'zam Hind*, 36.
[262] Some biographies assert that Shaykh Ibrāhīm ؑ studied the advanced books of Hadīth under Hazrat Muhaddith al-A'zam of Pakistan ؑ. However, this is historically inaccurate as the former

Along with Shaykh Hāmid ﷺ, other venerable scholars and teachers at the Dār al-'Ulūm instructed young Ibrāhīm in the *Siḥāḥ al-Sittah* (or, six major collections of Aḥādīth) and other books on rational theology (*Kalām*) as well. Shaykh Ibrāhīm ﷺ dedicated more than twelve years of his life to the pursuit of Sacred Knowledge gaining proficiency in an array of religious sciences with precision, diligence, and sincerity. Later in life he was honored with the honorific appellation *al-Mufassir al-A'zam Hind* (or, "The Greatest Exegetist of India") by the renowned *Mashā'ikh* of his time.[263]

Shaykh Ibrāhīm ﷺ was known for his piety, miracles, personal humility, and wisdom. He often said, "My own faults stop me from finding fault in others." And, "Piety is achieved through good character, not through filial ties." Thanks to his grandfather's supplications (*Du'ās*), Shaykh Ibrāhīm ﷺ outshined his contemporaries in challenging and refuting heretical sects. There is a profound link between A'lā Hazrat ﷺ and Shaykh Ibrāhīm ﷺ, one that is analogous in many ways to the special relationship that

---

completed his religious studies in the year 1344/1925 whilst the latter was still studying his secular sciences and had not yet completed the metric. Hazrat Muhaddith al-A'zam of Pakistan ﷺ visited the Dār al-'Ulūm in Bareilly with Shaykh Hāmid in 1934. For further discussion of this topic, see *Hayāt-e Mufassir-e A'zam Hind*, 37-38.

[263] Shaykh al-Muftī 'Abdul Wajid al-Qādirī, *Hayāt-e Mufassir-e A'zam Hind*, 11.

A Red-Letter Day

was developed between Imām Ahmad and his own grandfather, Mawlānā Razā 'Alī Khān ﷺ.

If Allah so wills Mawlānā Muhammad Kalīm al-Qādirī's forthcoming biography on Mufassir al-A'zam Hind will whet the inquiring reader's appetite. We must now turn our attention to the tumultuous period of the 1920s, in which, Imām Ahmad Razā Khān ﷺ was like a light in the firmament that guided the Community of Sayyidunā Muhammad ﷺ through an era when the traitor would be trusted and the trustworthy one in keeping the religion would be called a traitor.

Political Unrest in British India

In the early part of the 1920s, Mohandas K. Gandhi was advised to meet with Imām Ahmad ﷺ to discuss the Khilāfat movement (1919-1924). This issue was foremost in the minds of Indian Muslims, who were witnessing the tragic demise of the Ottoman Empire. A'lā Hazrat ﷺ was deeply concerned about the welfare of the Islamic Community. Accordingly, the scholars and Sufi saints affiliated to Bareilly Sharīf were sending as much aid as possible to Muslims in Turkey, the Middle East, and Africa. They were also imploring the Master of the Realm (*Mālik al-Mulk*) to ease the difficulties of those in the Ottoman Empire and grant them peace.[264] But there was very little that the Muslims of British India could do politically to change their condition. The Imām was cognizant of this fact and wary of those with an ulterior motive. He authored a book on the subject entitled, *Dawām*

---

[264] For further discussion of this topic, see Imām Ahmad Razā Khān, *Dawam al-'Aish fi'l Ummat min Quraysh*.

al-'Aish fi'l Ummat min Quraish [Persevering the Grandeur of the Quraish], to warn the Umma about those groups that sought to derail Indian Muslims through this temporal controversy. When he was told that Gandhi wished to speak with him, Imām Ahmad asked, "What would he speak about, religion or worldly affairs? If it is worldly affairs, what can I partake in, for I have abstained from the world and have no interest in it?"[265] The Khilāfat movement collapsed by 1924, but before its demise the organizers of this campaign began to distance themselves from Gandhi and the Indian National Congress.[266]

A'lā Hazrat ﷺ never lost sight of the Hereafter nor did he permit the realpolitik of home rule or controversies in the Islamic world to throw him off balance. He put first things first in accordance with the words of our Lord: *The life of the world is but distraction and play; while the Last Abode is indeed the Life, if they but knew.*[267] Allah reminds us about the vanity of this life, its mediocrity, its frustrations, and its brevity which is a constant Qur'ānic refrain, common to the earlier Revelations as well. The Book of Prophet Isaiah ﷺ says: *All nations before Him are as nothing; and they are*

---

[265] Shaykh 'Abdul Hakīm Sharaf al-Qādirī, *al-Baraylawiyyah Ka Tahqeeqi Tanqeedi Ja'iza* (Bhiwandi: Raza Islamic Foundation, n.d.), 242.
[266] See "Khilafat Movement," accessed on April 14, 2012, http://en.wikipedia.org/wiki/Khilafat_Movement#Collapse.
[267] Al-Qur'ān, 29:64.

counted to Him less than nothing, and vanity.²⁶⁸ More often than not, we are preoccupied by that which does not concern us, and lose sight of that which does.

Being a Traditionalist, Imām Ahmad never forsook the example set by our Prophet ﷺ. In consequence, the "temptations" (i.e., vices) of Western imperialism that were imposed upon colonized humanity thoroughly repulsed him. When Muslims began adopting Western fashion, for example, he retained his eloquent Islamic dress as a matter of principle and preference. For he was a faithful representative of the Beloved of Allah, Sayyidunā Muhammad ﷺ, whose very being was a reminder of the spiritual dignity of man on earth. A'lā Hazrat ؓ would only submit to the wishes of Allah and His Messenger ﷺ, and even failed to appear when summoned by the British Indian court in 1917. Those who are willing to defy unjust laws are few and far between, but rarer still is the man who surrenders his case completely to the Lord of the Highest Court. Allah the Exalted rewarded his faithful servant for his scrupulousness (*Wara'*) and absolute trust (*Tawakkul*), and within a few months the case was dismissed.²⁶⁹ *So rely on Allah, indeed Allah loves those who rely [on Him]*.²⁷⁰

---

²⁶⁸ 40:17.
²⁶⁹ Sanyal, *Ahmad Riza Khan Barelwi*, 120.
²⁷⁰ Al-Qur'ān, 3:159.

Political Unrest in British India

Indian Muslims were being pulled on all sides by the socio-political uproar surrounding them, but the situation went from worse to worst in the summer of 1920 when Mawlānā 'Abdul Barī added to the confusion by issuing a fatwā that called for mass emigration (*Hijrat*) to Muslim territories like Afghanistan.[271] These bewildering events led Imām Ahmad ؑ to sagaciously declare the nation an Abode of Peace (*Dār al-Islām*).[272] He asked the Umma residing in British India to live and let live, yet he also urged them to wean themselves away from the larger non-Muslim community by becoming as far as reasonably possible self-sufficient and self-reliant,[273] because this (over and above all other factors and considerations) would preserve their identity and give them lasting peace. He argued that social relations with the British were

---

[271] Usha Sanyal notes that, "**some twenty thousand people**—most of them Pathans from what is today the Northwest Frontier Province in Pakistan, but also peasants from the United Provinces and Sind—sold their possessions and marched toward Kabul. However, Amir Amanullah Khan (r. 1919-30) had just come to power in Afghanistan in the previous year... Fearing the economic consequences of the influx of so many people, Amanullah closed Afghanistan's frontiers to the emigrants, forcing most of them—**now destitute**—to go back to their homes" (*Ahmad Riza Khan Barelwi*, 81-82).

[272] See Imām Ahmad Razā Khān's *I'lām al-A'lām bi-anna Hindustān Dār al-Islām* [A Veritable Mountain of Knowledge Declares that India is an Abode of Peace].

[273] Imām Ahmad Razā Khān, "Islamic Economic Guidelines" [Tadbīre Falāh-o Najāt-o Islāh] in *Thesis of Imam Ahmad Raza* (Durban: Barkātur-Razā Publications, 2007), trans. Professor M.A. Qadrī, 457.

permissible in terms of earning a living and availing oneself of services provided by the British Indian government such as the railways, telegraph, and postal system as long as unbelief or disobedience to the Sharī'ah were not promoted thereby. He also pointed out some of the inherent inconsistencies of the Noncooperation movement (September 1920-February 1922), which was spearheaded unsuccessfully by Gandhi to induce the British government of India to grant self-rule (*Swarāj*) to the people of India,[274] for example, this movement continued to utilize the railways, telegraph, and postal system even though the proceeds were funding the very entity that they were trying to "quit" (i.e., the British Rāj).[275] The Indian Subcontinent was so embroiled in the struggle for independence that some political leaders and opportunists even called for *jihād* against the British, but A'lā Hazrat ﷺ in his *al-Mahajjat al-Mu'tamana fī Ayāt al-Mumtahanah* [The Middle Way in relation to the Verses of Sūrah al-Mumtahanah (or, "The Woman Tested")](1920) cautioned the Community against this by saying: "There is no Qur'ānic injunction that makes *jihād* obligatory for the Muslims of India, and he who holds the view that it is

---

[274] See the Encyclopaedia Britannica article "Non-Cooperation Movement," accessed on April 21, 2012, http://www.britannica.com/EBchecked/topic/417610/noncooperation-movement.
[275] Sanyal, *Ahmad Riza Khan Barelwi*, 110.

Political Unrest in British India

obligatory is an opponent of the Muslims and intends to harm them."[276] Being a farsighted scholar-saint, Imām Ahmad ﷺ wanted the Muslims of India to first change their own spiritual state by putting their trust in the All-Majestic Lord,[277] because *Allah does not change the condition of a people till they change themselves.*[278]

A'lā Hazrat ﷺ also knew that the country would definitely rid itself of English domination; and he anticipated the creation of a government along democratic lines. As fate would have it, one day during the month of Sha'bān in 1339/1920, he appointed Sadr ash-Sharī'at 'Allāma Amjad 'Alī al-Qādirī ﷺ (d.1367/1948), one of his foremost students and deputies, to be the Chief Judge of India (*Qadī al-Sha'rā*). 'Allāma Amjad ﷺ is the author of *Bahār-e Sharī'at* [Beautiful Effusions emanating from the Sacred Law], which is a comprehensive tome in seventeen volumes that covers almost every aspect of Islamic life.[279] The *Mujaddid* then turned to Shaykh Mustafā Razā Khān

---

[276] See *al-Mahajjat al-Mu'tamana fī Ayāt al-Mumtahana,* 208.
[277] Sanyal, *Ahmad Riza Khan Barelwi,* 79.
[278] Al-Qur'ān, 13:11.
[279] Volumes one (*Correct Beliefs*), two (*The Book of Purification*), and sixteen (*Islamic Morals and Etiquettes*) of this magnum opus have been translated into English by Mawlānā Muhammad Afthab Cassim. These works are available online at http://www.noori.org/UrseAalahazrat. html, and were released on the 'Urs of Imām Ahmad Razā Khān ﷺ on the 25th of Safar, 1433/2012. May Allah reward the translator for his steadfast service to the *Maslak,* Āmīn.

Reflections of Allah's Love

◈ and Mawlānā Muhammad Burhan al-Haqq ◈ from Jabalpurī and asked them to assist Sadr ash-Sharī'at as the Chief Muftīs of India (*al-Muftī al-Sha'rā*). A'lā Hazrat ◈ laid the foundation for the process of appointing an Islamic judge and muftī, so that no difficulty would be experienced after independence.[280] Thus the exoteric leadership for those following the *Ahl al-Sunnah wa al-Jamā'ah* in South Asia was established in Bareilly Sharīf on that fateful day.

Imām Ahmad Razā Khān al-Qādirī ◈ was constantly redressing the issues facing the Umma from without and within. Sunni scholars have historically defended the faith internally through giving lectures and writing treatises on the nature of heresy. In consequence, one will find the most self-conscious reflections on the nature of truth within the Islamic tradition in the writings of the renowned heresiologists of Sunnidom. Imām Ahmad's judicious pen is a representation of this inward looking propensity, and approach that was self-critical, and did not gloss over the fact that there are real fissures within the Umma. Unlike many contemporary Islamic scholars and reform movements, A'lā Hazrat ◈ was firm on who

---

[280] Sanyal, *Ahmad Riza Khan Barelwi*, 84-85.

the Sunnis are and what entails deviation from the Sunnah. His *esprit de corps* saw the People of the Sunnah through the darkness of dissension (*Fitna*) that the Trustworthy One (*al-Amīn*) ﷺ mentioned in the confirmed Ahādīth pertaining to the tribulations of the Last Days.

Hence, when an Islamic scholar asked Imām Ahmad ؓ why he was so severe on professed Muslims that disrespect the Prophet ﷺ, he replied, "O Mawlānā! I am severe upon those people because instead of insulting our Master, the Messenger of Allah ﷺ, I would rather they attack me and make me the target of their insults. I do not have any interest in what they say about me. At least, while they are busy insulting me, my beloved Master ﷺ is safe from their accursed words."[281]

Did Razā suffer loss of prestige,
 from the barbs that the detractors gave?
No, he preoccupied them,
 with slandering and insulting him,
 that the Beloved's name ﷺ might be saved!

Abū Hurayrah ؓ narrates that Allah's Messenger ﷺ has said: **"By the One who has my life in His hand, none of you will believe until he loves me more than his**

---

[281] Mawlānā Muhammad Afthab Cassim, *Imam Ahmad Raza*, 67-68.

Reflections of Allah's Love

father and his children."[282] Likewise Anas ﷺ relates that the Prophet ﷺ said: **"Whoever possesses three attributes will experience the sweetness of belief: that he loves Allah and His Messenger more than anything else; that he loves someone for the sake of Allah alone; and he hates reverting to disbelief as much as he would hate being thrown into a fire."**[283] Being an ardent lover of Allah and His Messenger ﷺ, A'lā Hazrat once said that if his heart were cleaved in two: one side would have *Lā ilāha illa-Allah*, and the other side would have the inscription *Muhammadun Rasūlu'llāh* ﷺ.[284] His words recall in particular the holy utterance (*Hadīth Qudsī*) of Allah Most Pure: **"Nothing contains Me, but the heart of My believing slave."**[285]

A'lā Hazrat's great-grandson, Muftī Mohammed Akhtār Razā Khān al-Qādirī al-Azharī (may Allah preserve him), appraised Imām Ahmad's love for the Prophet ﷺ with these words: "Love for the Prophet ﷺ was the prime focus of his life. All of his sayings and actions were steeped in love for the Prophet ﷺ that it can be said

---

[282] Al-Bukhārī ﷺ in his *Sahīh*, "The Book of Belief (*Īmān*)," trans. Ustādha Āisha Bewley, accessed on December 8, 2011, http://spl.qibla.com/Hadith/H0002P0002.aspx.
[283] Al-Bukhārī ﷺ in his *Sahīh*, "The Book of Belief (*Īmān*)."
[284] Imām Mustafā Razā Khān, *al-Malfūz al-Sharīf*, 3:420.
[285] This holy utterance, a long favorite among Sufis, is cited by Imām al-Ghazzālī in his *Ihyā' al-'Ulūm*, Imām al-Daylamī in his *Musnad al-Firdaws*, and Imām al-Suyutī in his *al-Durar al-Muntathirah*.

that, he was, from head to toe, immersed in the love of the Messenger of Allah ﷺ. Love of the Prophet ﷺ was his life and that was his message."²⁸⁶ Mawlānā Yasīn Akhtār Misbahī adds to Muftī Mohammed's appraisal of A'lā Hazrat ؓ by saying: "It is worth noting here that his love was not a kind of madness where all sense of judgment is lost; rather, his love bound him to comply with the wishes of the beloved ﷺ. This is the state of love, where a man's own wishes are vanquished and he becomes a follower of the wishes of his beloved. This is the state mentioned in the hadīth: **'that a man's desires are compliant with that [message] which I have come with.'** [*wa an yakunu hawāhu tab'an limā jiytu bihi*]. This aspect is reflected in all of his religious services and efforts."²⁸⁷

The Sublime Lord sent Imām Ahmad Razā Khān al-Qādirī ؓ to aid the Community of Sayyidunā Muhammad ﷺ by renewing our faith and love for the Chosen One ﷺ. The Exalted also taught the Muslim world how to love, respect, and venerate the noble Family of the Prophet

---

²⁸⁶ Mawlānā Yasīn Akhtār Misbahī, "Ahlu's Sunnah Wa'l Jama'ah: An Introduction," accessed on February 16, 2012, http://www.freewebs.com/barelwi/IntroToAhlusSunnah.pdf, 13.
²⁸⁷ Ibid.

Muhammad ﷺ through the words and deeds of His *Mujaddid*. Because love for the People of the House (*Ahl al-Bayt*) is an integral part of Sunni Islam;[288] and it is a subject that modern scholars should revisit with great fervor.

This fact is confirmed by the following narratives, once when A'lā Hazrat ؓ was traveling in a palanquin he caught the fragrant scent of a *Sayyid*,[289] which made him exclaim: "Bearers halt! Is there a Sayyid carrying this palanquin? I perceive the blessed scent of a Sayyid." After a moment's hesitation, one of the bearers came forward and answered in the affirmative. Imām Ahmad fell at his feet and begged for forgiveness. The Sayyid told A'lā Hazrat that he need not apologize, but the Imām continued imploring him and weeping, saying: "Please forgive me. What will I do on the Day of Judgment if the Holy Prophet ﷺ asks me about this incident, and he feels that my conduct was beneath the dignity of his noble Family?" Upon hearing these words of true love, the

---

[288] Sayyid al-Hāfiz Abū 'Abdullāh Muhammad ibn Ja'far al-Kattānī ؓ (d. 1345/1927) authored several outstanding works, including a collection of forty-two Ahādīth on the duty of loving Prophet Muhammad's ﷺ noble Family (which has recently been translated into English by Turath Publishing), as well as a three volume tome on the Prophet's ﷺ knowledge of the unseen, entitled *'Jalā al-Qulub min al-Asdā al-Gaybiyyah bi-Ihātatihi sall-Allāhu 'alayhi wa sallam bi al-Ulūm al-Kawniyyah* [Enlightening Hearts with Echoes of the Unseen by Explaining that He ﷺ Encompasses Worldly Knowledge].

[289] *Sayyid*: A descendent of our Master, Prophet Muhammad ﷺ.

Sayyid accepted A'lā Hazrat's apology, but much to his amazement, the Imām asked him to sit in the palanquin, as the scholar-saint carried the Prophet's ﷺ own flesh and blood throughout the city until he repaid the debt of each step the other had trodden.[290]

Every child from your pure lineage is a resplendent Light
Your essence is Light; and your household is a radiant Light.

According to another anecdote, it was A'lā Hazrat's wont to stand whenever he saw a certain child run past his front door. Sometimes this child would pass by his door ten times a day, and every single time the Imām immediately put aside his work and stood up out of respect for him. This, of course, was no ordinary child; he was a descendent of our Master Prophet Muhammad ﷺ.[291] Someone once asked Imām Ahmad ؓ how an Islamic judge should penalize a Sayyid, to which, he replied by saying: "He should not intend to punish the Sayyid. Rather, his intention must be that of someone who is removing a small quantity of mud that has fallen upon the Sayyid's feet. In other words, he is merely wiping off a speck of dirt."[292] Or perhaps it could be said that the Islamic judge is merely polishing the Sayyid's blessed

---

[290] Mawlānā Muhammad Afthab Cassim, *Imam Ahmad Raza*, 68-69.
[291] Ibid., 69.
[292] Ibid., 70.

Reflections of Allah's Love

shoes with utmost humility and *Ādāb*. Glory be to Allah, and all praise! 'Alī ibn Abī Tālib ﷺ relates that the Prophet ﷺ said: **"By Him in Whose hand is my soul, a slave will not have [true] belief until he loves me and he cannot love me until he loves my offspring."**[293] Ibn 'Adī, ad-Daylamī and Abū Nu'aym have reported on the authority of 'Alī ﷺ as well that the Prophet ﷺ said: **"The most firm of you on the *Sirāt*[294] will be those who most dearly love my Household and my Companions."**[295]

How accurately Carl W. Ernst and Bruce B. Lawrence note in *Sufi Martyrs of Love: The Chishti Order in South Asia and Beyond* that the devotional and pietist Barelwī school,[296]

---

[293] Sayyid al-Hāfiz Abū 'Abdullāh Muhammad ibn Ja'far al-Kattānī, *al-Arba'īn: On the Duty of Loving the Family of the Prophet Muhammad* ﷺ (London: Turath Publishing, 2010), trans. Safaruk Zaman Chowdhury, 51.

[294] The *Sirāt* is a bridge that is placed over the Fire of Hell, which the believers must cross to enter the Garden.

[295] Sayyid al-Hāfiz Abū 'Abdullāh Muhammad ibn Ja'far al-Kattānī, *al-Arba'īn: On the Duty of Loving the Family of the Prophet Muhammad* ﷺ, 57.

[296] Imām Ahmad ﷺ is highly revered as the leader of the *Ahl al-Sunnah wa al-Jamā'ah* in modern South Asian Islam; Islamicists tend to refer to his pedagogy as the Barelwī school due to his surname *al-Barelwī*, which indicates his place of birth [i.e., Bareilly, India]. However, the reader should note that opponents of the *Ahl al-Sunnah* use the word "Barelwī" in a derogatory sense to cast aspersions upon Imām Ahmad's school of thought.

"champions practices that honor the Prophet and the Sufi saints."[297] Imām Ahmad's pedagogy is one of reverential love for Allah and His Messenger ﷺ. His life is like a mirror reflecting Allah's love upon the Community of Sayyidunā Muhammad ﷺ, as our Prophet ﷺ himself has said: **"The faithful is the mirror of the Faithful [al-mu'minu mir'ātu 'l-Mu'min]"**[298] Al-Ghawth al-A'zam Sultān al-Awliyā' Sayyidunā ash-Shaykh Muhyi'd-dīn 'Abdul Qādir al-Jīlānī ﷺ elucidates the mystical meaning of this noble utterance in his *The Book of the Secret of Secrets* [Kitāb Sirr al-Asrār], "The first 'faithful' is the heart of the faithful servant, while the second is Allah (Exalted is He). Allah has described Himself (Exalted is He) as: *The Faithful, the Guardian [u] 'l-Mu'minu 'l-Muhaiminu* (59:23). The final abode of this group is in the third Garden, which is Paradise [*Firdaws*]."[299]

Al-Munawī, on the other hand, has commented upon the literal meaning of this Hadīth Sharīf, **"The believer is the mirror of the believer,"**[300] by saying: "In a mirror, man sees nothing but his own face and person. And if he exerts

---

[297] Carl W. Ernst and Bruce B. Lawrence, *Sufi Martyrs of Love: The Chishti Order in South Asia and Beyond* (New York: PALGRAVE MACMILLAN, 2002), 96.
[298] Shaykh 'Abdul Qādir al-Jīlānī, *The Book of the Secret of Secrets and the Manifestation of Lights* (Fort Lauderdale: Al-Baz Publishing, Inc., 2000), trans. Muhtar Holland, 23.
[299] Ibid., 24.
[300] Narrated by Abū Dāwūd and others.

himself to the utmost in order to see the body of the mirror, he does not see it because his own image veils him. Al-Tibi said: 'Concerning the unveiling of his brother's defects, the (examined) believer is like a polished mirror which displays all images reflected in it, no matter how minute...' Therefore whoever has gathered the features of Iman, accomplished the manners of Islam, and excelled internally against the blameworthy features of his ego (*nafs*), then his heart raises to the peak of *ihsan* (excellence), so pure that it becomes like a mirror; if the believers look at him, they see the darkness of their own condition reflected within the purity of his, and they see the ill state of their own manners reflected within the excellence of his."[301]

Love for the Imām ﷺ is a clear sign that the lover is from the *Ahl al-Sunnah wa al-Jamā'ah*, just as opposition to him is indicative of one who surreptitiously or openly disdains certain essentials of the Sunni creed. The veritable Deobandī apologetic, "Iman, Kufr, and Takfir" written by Nuh Keller in 2007, is a prime example of a surreptitious attack on A'lā Hazrat ﷺ.[302] This insidious

---

[301] Al-Munawī in his *Fayd al-Qadīr* (6:251-252, #9141-9142) as quoted in *al-Musuat al-islami aqida ahl al-sunnah wa al-jamaat*, 1:21-22.

[302] Shaykh Monawwar Ateeq has written a number of excellent articles dealing with this subject, including "Explaining the Correct Methodology of Imam Subki in *Takfir*," "A Rejoinder Contextualizing the Hadiths Quoted by Shaykh Nuh in *Iman, Kufr, and Takfir*,"

essay can be juxtaposed with Ehsān Ilahī Zahīr's more conspicuous attack on the Imām ﷺ and Sufism in his controversial book, *al-Baraylawiyya* [The Barelwīs]. According to authoritative scholars from the Arab world, Zahīr is "an unadulterated an outright Wahhābī"[303] and "a rabid anti-Sufi."[304] Serious Muslims should read Shaykh Khālid Thābit's *Insāf al-Imām* [The Justice of the Imām],[305] and Muftī Mohammed Akhtār Razā Khān al-Qādirī al-Azharī's *al-Haqīqat al-Baraylawiyya* [The Reality of the Barelwīs], also known as *Mira'at al-Najdīyya*. The former work is probably one of the best biographies on A'lā Hazrat ﷺ written in Arabic by a Sunni scholar from Egypt. Ihsanica Media has recently published a fine English translation of *Insāf al-Imām*, entitled *A Just Word: The Life & Legacy of Imām Ahmad Ridā Khān al-Barelwī*. Muftī Mohammed's *al-Haqqīqat al-Baraylawiyya* is an effective rebuttal to Ehsān Ilahī Zahīr's slander and calumny. It is

---

"Knowledge of the Unseen Theology: Arguments on the Scope of Prophetic Knowledge," and a work in Urdu-Arabic entitled, "Do Asha'ris Believe Allah Can Lie." All of these essays are available at http://scholarsink.wordpress.com/.

[303] See Shaykh Khālid Thābit's "Foreword" to *A Just Word: The Life & Legacy of Imām Ahmad Ridā Khān al-Barelwī*.

[304] Shaykh Gibril Fouad Haddad, "Replies to Some of Ihsan Ilahi Zahir's Attacks on Imam Ahmad Rida Khan al-Barelwi," accessed on May 15, 2012, http://www.livingislam.org/n/riiz_e.html.

[305] Ihsanica Media (http://ihsanica.com/) hopes to release this title in the summer of 2012.

Reflections of Allah's Love

currently available in Arabic from Dār al-Muqattam in Cairo, Egypt.

There are some who are fortunate enough to look upon Imām Ahmad Razā Khān al-Qādirī ﷺ with the eyes of an ardent lover, because they see in him the mirror of Allah (*al-mu'minu mir'ātu 'l-Mu'min*); and there are those mean-spirited souls who try to dissuade the lover from his obsessive love, since all they can see, in the mirror of the faithful believer, is the darkness of their own condition that is reflected within the purity of his, and the ill state of their own manners reflected within the excellence of his. May the Faithful bless us with eyes that see His reflection in the faithful, and may the Guardian of Faith protect us from those who are *deaf, dumb and blind*,[306] Āmīn and Āmīn.

---

[306] Al-Qur'ān, 2:18.

Glad Tidings

Four months and twenty days before he attained union, Imām Ahmad ؓ deduced the date of his passing (*Wisāl*) from the Qur'ānic verse: *And there shall be passed around them silver vessels and goblets.*[307] As the hour drew nigh he requested all those at home to forgive any shortcomings on his part, and obliged them to tell those not present to forgive him as well. On hearing these words, his loved ones began to weep, for they knew his time was at hand. He specifically told his family that no photos with animate objects should be near him. They were to recite Sūrah Yā Sīn, Sūrah ar-Ra'd, and send salutations and blessings upon the Prophet ﷺ at his bedside. Mourners were to be kept away from him, and his ritual bath (*Ghusl*) was to be in accordance with the Sunnah. His funeral prayer was to be led by either: Hujjat al-Islām Shaykh Hāmid Razā Khān ؓ, or in his absence, by, Sadr ash-Sharī'at 'Allāma Amjad 'Alī al-Qādirī ؓ. He did not want the funeral to be delayed for any reason, and asked that the pallbearers recite *Kā be*

---

[307] Al-Qur'ān, 76:15.

kī badru duja (or, "O the full moon of the Ka'ba in the darkness of the night"), nor did he want anything read in his praise. He wanted his grave-clothes (*Kafan*) to be in accordance with the Sunnah, and the food from his *Fateha* distributed amongst the poor. His final advise to his brethren was: "Remain steadfast on the religion of Islam; do not leave the Path of Sharī'ah, and stick to the religion (*al-Dīn*) that I followed [meaning: the *Ahl al-Sunnah wa al-Jamā'ah*]."

Our Prophet ﷺ has said: **"My Community [*Umma*] will split up into seventy-three sects,"**[308] and that every one of them will be in error, apart from one solitary exception namely the People of the Prophetic Way and the Majority of Scholars. Imām Ahmad's parting advice is an implicit warning against the seventy-two sects within the Islamic Community that are in error and astray, and an admonishment to his followers to follow the People of the Sunnah that constitute one single group or denomination (*Tā'ifa*). That is why he uses the word *al-Dīn*, or "the religion," in a slightly different sense; he first mentions the religion of Islam in general, and then alludes to the belief and methodology of traditional Sunni Islam in particular. He followed the Hanafī school of Islamic law, and asked his students and disciples to do the same.

---

[308] Shaykh 'Abdul Qādir al-Jīlānī, *Sufficient Provision for Seekers of the Path of Truth*, 1:393.

Glad Tidings

A'lā Hazrat ﷺ returned to the Realm of Divine Beauty on Friday, the 25th of Safar, 1340 AH (October 28, 1921). It was the exact time of the Friday call to prayer. Thus his absence from the scene made the world a poorer place, but in the course of the period of mourning, his devoted followers were surprised to receive glad tidings from an unexpected guest. Far away in the land of Shām,[309] a Sufi saint from Jerusalem (*Bayt al-Maqdis*) dreamt of Prophet Muhammad ﷺ, and in his dream, many of the noble Companions were seated around the Messenger of Allah ﷺ waiting for someone to arrive. So the Palestinian saint inquired: "O Messenger of Allah ﷺ! Who are you expecting?" The Prophet ﷺ replied: "Ahmad Razā Khān." The venerable Sufi saint then asked: "Who is Ahmad Razā Khān?" And the Last Prophet ﷺ answered: "A scholar from Bareilly." When the Palestinian awoke, he left Jerusalem and journeyed to Bareilly Sharīf to meet with A'lā Hazrat ﷺ, but much to his dismay, the great scholar,

---

[309] *Al-Shām*, or the greater Levant region, is one of the most blessed lands on earth. It includes the lands of present-day Syria, Palestine, Lebanon, and Jordan from the Euphrates to Sinai. Imām an-Nawawī ﷺ wrote a book on the merits of Shām, entitled *Fadā'īl Shām*. Another excellent work on this subject is *The Immense Merits of Al-Shām* by the late Grand Shaykh of Mecca, al-Sayyid Muhammad ibn 'Alawī al-Mālikī ﷺ (d. 1425/2004). Shaykh Muhammad passed away on a Friday, the 15th of Ramadan, in the ennobled city of Mecca. May Allah have mercy on him and fill his grave with light, Āmīn.

that the Prophet ﷺ himself had spoken of in his dream, had already made his "divine appointment."³¹⁰

Lovers of Imām Ahmad ؓ say that his soul went to Medina the Illumined to be near the Prophet ﷺ. This narration is based on A'lā Hazrat's own words: "My time is near and India is India, but I do not even feel like passing away in Mecca the Ennobled. My desire is that I should pass away with faith in the illumined city of Medina, and then be laid to rest in 'The Garden of Heaven' (*Jannat al-Baqī'*). Verily, Allah is All-Powerful."³¹¹ One might ask why then visit the tomb of any Sufi saint if the occupant of the grave has in fact vacated the premises? What must be understood here is that the soul of an ordinary believer,³¹² let alone the Friends of Allah and His Prophets cannot be confined to the physical diminishes of a grave, in fact, the gravesites are worthy of pilgrimage chiefly because a part of the spirituality (*Rūhāniyya*) of the great saints is concentrated at their resting place, and this

---

³¹⁰ Mawlānā Muhammad Afthab Cassim, *Imam Ahmad Raza*, 114-115. Hāfiz al-Millat Shaykh 'Abdul 'Azīz Muhaddith Mubarakpurī ؓ (1312-1396/1894-1976) met an Imām in Ajmer Sharīf that came across this Palestinian Shaykh.
³¹¹ Ibid., 115.
³¹² Imām Ahmad Razā Khān ؓ in yet another masterpiece titled *Return of the Souls* explains how the spirits of the dead return to their homes on the eve of every Friday and other special occasions, and that they are free to travel in the Intermediate Realm (*Barzakh*) between death and the resurrection. This is supported by various narrations.

Glad Tidings

then continues to provide untold benedictions and blessings to the visitor. It goes without saying that the blessings gathered by the pilgrim are dependent upon the station of the saint and the devotees own faith.[313] And Allah knows best.

The blessed mausoleum of Imām Ahmad Razā Khān al-Qādirī ﷺ in Bareilly, India is still a place of pious visitation. Every year on the 25th of Safar, throngs of people from around the world attend the anniversary of his union with the Beloved ('Urs). May Allah sanctify his lofty secret and fill his grave with light.

May the Sublime Lord grant us enabling success to practice, experience, and lovingly impart to all men what his impeccable legacy means to this Umma and the world, Āmīn and Āmīn.

---

[313] Sayyid Abu'l Husain Ahmad an-Nūrī ﷺ in *Horizons of Perfection* identifies two types of answers that a living person may receive at the mausoleum (*Mazār*) of a Sufi saint: one is a correct feeling, and the other is an audible sound. However, he further points out that the Friends of Allah experience such states through clairvoyance, or spiritual insight. For further discussion of this topic, see the twenty-first nūr in the third luster, "Concerning Tasawwuf."

Al-Arba'īn

From Abū 'd-Dardā' ﷺ we learn that someone once said: "O Messenger of Allah ﷺ, what must one do to become a person of knowledge (*Faqīh*)?" The Prophet ﷺ answered him by saying: **"Whosoever memorizes forty narrations for my nation in matters of its religion, Allah shall resurrect him on the Day of Judgment as a scholar and I shall be an intercessor and witness for him."**[314] 'Alī ibn Abī Tālib ﷺ, 'Abdullāh ibn Mas'ūd ﷺ, Mu'ādh ibn Jabal ﷺ, Ibn 'Umar ﷺ, Ibn 'Abbās ﷺ, Anas ibn Mālik ﷺ, Abū Hurayrah ﷺ, and Abū Sa'īd al-Khudrī ﷺ narrated this Hadīth Sharīf.

Imām Ahmad Razā Khān al-Qādirī ﷺ gathered forty narrations on the Prophet's intercession ﷺ (*Shafā'at*) in obeisance to the above Hadīth Sharīf. He also chose this meritorious topic because the Muslims of India had begun to question the authenticity of our Prophet's *Shafā'at*, which is a well-attested belief among Sunnis. He said that

---

[314] Muftī Jalāl ad-Dīn Ahmad al-Qādirī al-Amjadī, *In Light of the Sacred Traditions of the Beloved* ﷺ, 84.

Al-Arba'īn

the question itself was a sign of the proximity of the Hour.[315]

He aptly named this work *Ismā' al-Arba'īn fi Shafā'ati Sayyid Al-Mahbūbīn* ﷺ [Hear the Forty Traditions on the Intercession of the Master of the Beloveds ﷺ]. Before quoting a single Prophetic Tradition he would mention the name of Allah's Messenger ﷺ in the most reverential fashion by reiterating his name and title thus: "the Holy Prophet ﷺ, the Intercessor of the Sinners ﷺ, has said" or "our Beloved Prophet ﷺ, the Intercessor of the Sinners ﷺ, said."[316]

All praise belongs to Allah alone, who blessed this Umma with a Renewer (*Mujaddid*) that conscientiously multiplied the reward (*Sawāb*) of his work in this fashion. A'lā Hazrat ؓ ensured that the spiritual rank of his readers was elevated in this life and the next, for he never lost sight of the Prophet's words ﷺ: **"Whoever invokes a single blessing (salutation) upon me, Allah sends ten blessings upon him."**[317] Imagine the *Sawāb* of this marvelous work that combines the former and latter Prophetic Traditions!

---

[315] Imām Ahmad Razā Khān, "Forty Ahādīth on the Intercession of the Holy Prophet Muhammad ﷺ" in *Thesis of Imam Ahmad Raza* ؓ (Durban, Barkātur-Razā Publications, 2007), trans. Shaykh 'Abdul Hādī, 91.
[316] Ibid., 98ff.
[317] Muftī Jalāl ad-Dīn Ahmad al-Qādirī al-Amjadī, *In Light of the Sacred Traditions of the Beloved* ﷺ, 161.

Reflections of Allah's Love

May Allah the Exalted open our hearts and minds to the genius and devotion of His slave, who rekindled our love for His Beloved ﷺ and safeguarded our creed from the people of falsehood, Āmīn.

What follows are forty-four narrations[318] of the Chosen One ﷺ that Imām Ahmad Razā Khān al-Qādirī ؓ embodied through his strict adherence to the letter and spirit of the Prophetic Sunnah. It is hoped that after reading these Ahādīth the reader's love for Allah's Beloved ﷺ and His elite servant ؓ will increase.

Hadīth Sharīf 1
"Richness does not lie in many possessions; richness is the richness of the soul."

Hadīth Sharīf 2
"Fast and you will get well."

Hadīth Sharīf 3
"Name yourselves with my name but do not use my kunya."

---

[318] The author has included four additional narrations to make it an uneven multiple of eleven which, of course, is a number that holds special significance in the Qādirī Tarīqah. **Nota Bene:** Citations for the Ahādīth listed here may be found by going back through the text.

Al-Arba'īn

Hadīth Qudsī 4
"Whosoever disrespects a friend (*Walī*) of Mine, I declare war on him."

Hadīth Sharīf 5
"Modesty is a branch of faith."

Hadīth Qudsī 6
"Allah the Exalted has said: 'All good deeds of the son of Adam are multiplied ten to seven hundredfold, except fasting, for it is Mine, and I shall reward a man for it, for he has left his appetite, his food and drink for My sake!'"

Hadīth Sharīf 7
"You must follow the exemplary traditional practices [*sunan*] of those who have gone before you, by treading in their very footsteps. You must take exactly the same course as the one they took, inch by inch, cubit by cubit, span by span, to the extent that if they had ever entered a lizard's lair, you would enter it too."

Hadīth Sharīf 8
"The keeper of my Sunnah at the time my Community has lapsed into corruption will receive the reward of a hundred martyrs."

Reflections of Allah's Love

Hadīth Sharīf 9
"Marriage is my exemplary way [*sunnatī*]; whoever loves my character [*fitratī*] should follow my example."

Hadīth Sharīf 10
"The world is an asset and the best asset of the world is a pious woman."

Hadīth Sharīf 11
"Marry and multiply, then I shall glory in you before the nations on the Day of Resurrection: [in all of you,] even the miscarried fetus."

Hadīth Sharīf 12
"The most perfect of the believers in faith is he who has the best character, and is most gentle toward his family."

Hadīth Sharīf 13
"My eyes sleep but my heart does not sleep."

Hadīth Sharīf 14
"When the night of mid-Sha'bān arrives, Allah makes careful scrutiny of His creatures, then He forgives the true believers, gives respite to the unbelievers, and

Al-Arba'īn

leaves the resentful to their resentment until they call for Him."

Hadīth Sharīf 15
"One who [sincerely] repents from sin is like one who has not sinned."

Hadīth Sharīf 16
"None of you greets me except that Allah returns my soul unto me and I return his greeting."

Hadīth Sharīf 17
"The Prophets are alive in their grave performing the ritual prayer (*Salāt*)."

Hadīth Sharīf 18
"Allah, the Exalted, has forbidden the earth from consuming the bodies of the Prophets!"

Hadīth Sharīf 19
"Glory be to Him who has brought this (vehicle) under our control though we were unable to control it. Surely, we are to return to our Lord."

Reflections of Allah's Love

Hadīth Qudsī 20
"My slave does not draw closer to Me with anything more beloved to Me than that which I have made obligatory upon him. My slave continues to draw closer with supererogatory acts of devotion until I love him. When I love him, I am his hearing with which he hears, his sight with which he sees, his hand with which he grasps and his foot with which he walks. If he asks Me I will definitely give him, and if he seeks refuge with Me I will definitely give him refuge."

Hadīth Sharīf 21
"Go in the Name of Allah and fight the enemy. But do not kill the elderly, children, or women. Do not be transgressors, for Allah loves those who keep the highest standards of discipline and do not harm people (*Muhsinīn*)."

Hadīth Sharīf 22
"Surely, Allah will send for this Umma at the advent of every one hundred years a person (or persons) who will renew its religion for it."

Al-Arba'īn

Hadīth Sharīf 23
"The ink of the scholar is dearer than the blood of the martyr; on the Day of Resurrection, the former shall be weighed against the latter and outweigh it."

Hadīth Sharīf 24
"Do not do to others that which you would not want others to do to you."

Hadīth Sharīf 25
"The example between you and me is like a camel that breaks loose and runs away. The owner of the camel says, 'Leave it! I know what it needs.' He then offers the camel an olive branch, which it considers from a safe distance. The owner approaches the disturbed camel slowly, and convinces it to rest. Thereafter, the owner mounts his camel and guides it home."

Hadīth Sharīf 26
"All creatures are Allah's dependents, and the most beloved of creation to Allah is the one who is benevolent to His dependents."

Hadīth Sharīf 27
"The best of you is the one who is the most helpful to others."

Hadīth Sharīf 28

"Run away from them (meaning: those who deviate from the Sunnah) and keep them away from you, so that they do not mislead you."

Hadīth Sharīf 29

"The counsel I bequeath to you is dutiful devotion [*taqwā*] to Allah, and paying heed and obedience [to your leader], even if he happens to be an Abyssinian slave, for anyone who lives on after me will experience much disharmony. You must therefore strive to follow my exemplary practice [*sunnatī*], and the exemplary practice of the rightly guided Caliphs [*sunnat al-khulafā' ar-rāshidīn*] after I am gone. You must hold on to it with a very tight grip, and doggedly sink your teeth into it. You must beware of novel fashions [*muhdathāt al-umūr*], for every novelty is a heretical innovation [*bid'a*], and every heretical innovation is a deviation from the right path."

Hadīth Sharīf 30

"Recite the Qur'ān for it will be light for you on the earth and a treasure for you in the heaven."

Hadīth Sharīf 31

"Paradise lies at the mother's feet."

Al-Arba'īn

Hadīth Sharīf 32
Abū Hurayrah ﷺ narrates that a person asked the Prophet ﷺ: "Who has the greatest claim on me with regard to service and kind treatment?" The Prophet ﷺ replied: "Your mother, and again your mother, and once again your mother. After her is the claim of your father."

Hadīth Sharīf 33
"The first of those to enter the Garden of Paradise will be those who are constantly praising Allah [*al-hammādūna li'llāh*]."

Hadīth Qudsī 34
"I am to my servant as he expects of Me, I am with him when he remembers Me. If he remembers Me in his heart, I remember him to Myself, and if he remembers me in an assembly, I mention him in an assembly better than his."

Hadīth Sharīf 35
"The believer with the most perfect faith is the one who has the best character and the one who is kindest to his wife."

Hadīth Sharīf 36
"By the One who has my life in His hand, none of you will believe until he loves me more than his father and his children."

Hadīth Sharīf 37
"Whoever possesses three attributes will experience the sweetness of belief: that he loves Allah and His Messenger more than anything else; that he loves someone for the sake of Allah alone; and he hates reverting to disbelief as much as he would hate being thrown into a fire."

Hadīth Qudsī 38
"Nothing contains Me, but the heart of My believing slave."

Hadīth Sharīf 39
"None of you is a [perfect] believer until his desires are compliant with that [message] which I have come with."

Hadīth Sharīf 40
"By Him in Whose hand is my soul, a slave will not have [true] belief until he loves me and he cannot love me until he loves my offspring."

Al-Arba'īn

Hadīth Sharīf 41

"The most firm of you on the *Sirāt* will be those who most dearly love my Household and my Companions."

Hadīth Sharīf 42

"The faithful is the mirror of the Faithful [*al-mu'minu mir'ātu 'l-Mu'min*]"

Hadīth Sharīf 43

"The believer is the mirror of the believer."[319]

Hadīth Sharīf 44

"My Community [*Umma*] will split up into seventy-three sects, and the sect that will cause the greatest mischief for my Community will be the one made up of people who use their own subjective opinion [*ra'y*] as the standard by which to assess affairs. They will declare what is lawful to be illegal [*yuharrimūna'l-halāl*], and they will legitimize that which is unlawful [*yuhallilūna'l-harām*]."

---

[319] This Hadīth Sharīf appears twice since it is interpreted in two different ways; the first being esoteric while the latter is exoteric.

Milestones in the Life of A'lā Hazrat ﷺ

NINETEENTH CENTURY

1272/1856   Imām Ahmad Razā Khān ﷺ is born in the city of Bareilly, India.

1273/1857   The Indian Revolt is lost to the British Empire, who seized control over the vast tracks of the Indian Subcontinent.

1285/1869   Imām Ahmad completes his Islamic education at the age of thirteen and issues his first religious edict.

1291/1875   A'lā Hazrat marries Sayyidah Irshād Begum ﷺ. They are blessed with two sons and five daughters as time goes by.

1292/1876   Hujjat al-Islām Shaykh Hāmid Razā Khān ﷺ is born.

Milestones in the Life of A'lā Hazrat ؑ

1293/1876 'Allāma Naqī 'Alī Khān and his son are initiated into the Qādirī Tarīqah, and given authorization to impart Sufism to others by Sayyid Shāh Āl-e Rasūl ؑ of Marehra Sharīf.

1296/1879 Imām Ahmad ؑ undertakes his first Pilgrimage, accompanied by his noble parents. Here he is recognized and blessed with licenses from venerable scholar-saints from the Hanafī and Shāfi'ī schools of Islamic jurisprudence.

1297/1880 'Allāma Naqī 'Alī ؑ attains union.

1310/1892 Muftī al-A'zam Hind Shaykh Mustafā Razā Khān ؑ is born and blessed by Sayyid Shāh Abu'l Husain Ahmad an-Nūrī ؑ of Marehra Sharīf. Years later, Shaykh Mustafā compiled *al-Malfūz al-Sharīf* [The Noble Vocals (of A'lā Hazrat ؑ)] into a colossal four volume tome that contains wisdom, anecdotes, and extemporaneous advice.

173

TWENTIETH CENTURY (TO 1921)

1318/1900 A'lā Hazrat ﷺ is declared a *Mujaddid* in South Asia by the 'Ulamā of the *Ahl al-Sunnah wa al-Jamā'ah*.

1398/1901 *Kanz al-Īmān fī Tarjuma al-Qur'ān* [A Treasury of Faith pertaining to the Translation of the Qur'ān] is published and distributed for the benefit of South Asian Muslims. This work is an authoritative interpretation of the Speech of Allah into the Urdu language.[320]

1323/1905 Imām Ahmad spontaneously commenced his monumental second Hajj, and received numerous endorsements and accolades from the scholar-saints of the Meccan and Medinan Sanctuaries (*Haramayn Sharīf*) including the title *Mujaddid* of the 14th Islamic century and the *Mujaddid* of the Umma.

---

[320] The author gives special emphasis to this work amongst all of the Imām's wonderful treatises, because her honorable Murshid al-Kālim recommended it as quite simply the best translation of the Glorious Qur'ān in the Urdu language and a sure source of guidance and light.

Milestones in the Life of A'lā Hazrat ﷺ

1325/1907 Shaykh Ibrāhīm Razā Khān ﷺ is born, and Imām Ahmad ﷺ hosts an extraordinary feast to mark the occasion.

1329/1911 Imām Ahmad blesses his four year old grandson (Shaykh Ibrāhīm ﷺ) with spiritual successorship and authorization in all the Sufi orders. He also announces to all those present that his grandson will become his foremost spokesman.

1339/1920 A'lā Hazrat ﷺ turned down an offer to meet with Gandhi to discuss the Khilāfat movement (1919-1924), and wrote several books on how to preserve the identity of Sunnis in an Abode of Peace (*Dār al-Islām*), the importance of changing our own condition, and holding fast to the People of the Sunnah, as a spiritual remedy to the crisis facing the Umma in South Asia at that time. With independence on the horizon and his hour nigh, A'lā Hazrat ﷺ appointed one of his foremost students and deputies Sadr ash-Sharī'at 'Allāma Amjad 'Alī al-Qādirī ﷺ (d.1367/1948) to be the Chief Judge of India (*Qadī al-Sha'rā*) in the blessed month of Sha'bān. He then turned to Shaykh Mustafā Razā Khān ؓ and Mawlānā Muhammad Burhan al-Haqq ؓ, and asked them to assist Sadr ash-Sharī'at as the Chief Muftīs of India (*al-Muftī al-Sha'rā*).

1340/1921 His Eminence, Imām Ahmad Razā Khān al-Qādirī ؓ, attained union on the 25th of Safar. He entered this world on a Monday at the time of the Zuhr prayer, and he left it on a Friday at the exact time of the Jumu'ah Adhān. All praise belongs to Allah alone, the Lord of the Worlds, and may endless peace and blessings be upon our Beloved Messenger Muhammad, Mercy to the Worlds, and upon his noble Kin and illustrious Companions.

www.ingramcontent.com/pod-product-compliance
Lightning Source LLC
LaVergne TN
LVHW041251080426
835510LV00009B/687